AF559927

A CRITICAL STUDY OF THE NOVELS OF ANITA DESAI

N.R. GOPAL

PUBLISHERS & DISTRIBUTORS (P) LTD

Published by

ATLANTIC

PUBLISHERS & DISTRIBUTORS (P) LTD

7/22, Ansari Road, Darya Ganj,
New Delhi-110002
Phones : +91-11-40775252, 23273880, 23275880, 23280451
Fax : +91-11-23285873
Web : www.atlanticbooks.com
E-mail : orders@atlanticbooks.com

Branch Office
5, Nallathambi Street, Wallajah Road,
Chennai-600002
Phones : +91-44-64611085, 32413319
E-mail : chennai@atlanticbooks.com

Printed in India at Nice Printing Press, A-33/3A, Site-IV,
Industrial Area, Sahibabad, Ghaziabad, U.P.

Dedicated to

Father and Mother
Under whose loving care
I learnt the first lessons
of the alphabet...

FOREWORD

Indian English Fiction has decidedly taken many strides forward ever since it started. The pioneers Mulk Raj Anand, R.K. Narayan, Raja Rao and Bhabani Bhattacharya laid the foundations of narrative which captured the Indian landscape in its multifarious variety and vivacity. Some of these pioneers have derived inspiration from the older narrative methods combining them with their own methods locally derived and invented. Raja Rao, for example, follows the Puranic method relying upon the levels of narration-meaning complexes. This mode of narration often leads to the allegorical method. Mulk Raj Anand and R.K. Narayan rely more upon the empirical-symbolical mode of the existence of the narrative. They do not necessarily take a mythological structure and breed their characters and situations into it. The local tale is more important in them.

Modernism has played a great role in shaping the second generation of Indian English novelists. Since modernism came rather late in India, it has manifested itself, as far as creative writers are concerned, in the dessociation of sensibility, fragmented vision, and the feelings of anxiety, nausia, boredom have all been part of the characters round whom the stories are woven. This is particularly so among the female novelists. Kamala Markandeya, Ruth Prawer Jhabavala, Atiya Hussain, Anita Desai, and more recently, Dina Mehta, have all depicted a distinct female sensibility at work in the perception as well as the representation of reality.

Novel is a recent evolution compared to other genres of literature. However, the novels serve as a link between the older narratives and the newer versions of the representation of reality. The monumental studies of narratology by Eric Auerbach (*Mimesis*) and E.R. Curtius (*European Literature and the Latin Middle Ages*) serve as great pointers to the study of Greek and Latin literatures before European renaissance. In the Indian context, the renaissance came fairly late; moreover, it was regional in nature. The process of awakening was generated particularly by those Indian English creative writers who had lived abroad for quite some time and had the two worlds at their disposal to write about India and the country they visited. This bifocal dimension to Indian writing in English is very important in the resurgence of the manner and the method of story-telling.

Anita Desai (1937—) is a very distinguished and distinct female novelist from the rest of her generation's other female novelists. In her novels Indian English fiction has acquired a depth which it seldom had before. Whereas other female novelists concentrate upon a linear path which shows the development of a story in a causal sequence, Anita Desai writes in the symbolic mode which not only subordinates plot to the other character but also pushes it to the background. Linear and progressive plots make for a story that is apprehensible, perceptible and representable. This is true of Nayantara Sahgal, Ruth Jhabavala and Dina Mehta where one empirical detail is loaded upon another to create a pattern of human belief. Even Arun Joshi, who resorts to the symbolic mode in *The River and the City* is symbolic mostly at the structural level. Anita Desai's novels have a structure (if at all) which defies itself, for her characters exist in a tensional relationship to the situation, plot and the establishment which is the backbone of the whole network of relationships. A number of critical studies have appeared on the novels of Anita Desai. Madhusudan Prasad studies characters in the light of existentialism in Anita Desai's novels; Usha Bande and Jasbir Jain study the psychological aspects of characters. Ramchandra Rao studies the poetic and lyrical aspect of her novels.

R.S. Singh, G.P. Sharma, B.O. Vyas and a few others have all commented upon Anita Desai's fiction following a thematic (Non-Dialectical) approach. This leaves a major area to be explored — the fictional technique of Anita Desai. Dr. N. Raj Gopal Rao has filled this gap by studying this aspect of her novels remarkably well. Not a linguist by training or profession, Dr. Gopal has ventured into a new field and brings to light many of the hitherto unexplored aspects of Anita Desai's style and method. Anita Desai herself has said :

> My writing is an effort to discover, underline and convey the significance of things. I must sieze upon that incomplete and seemingly meaningless mass of reality around me and try and

discover its significance by plunging below the surface and plumbing the depths, then illuminating those depths till they become more lucid, brilliant, explicable reflection of the visible world.

This explains the measure of the cross-referentiality of the character. For Anita Desai, autobiography and biography may or may not play their part in the formation of characters and situations, for a talented writer can imagine so much. Autobiography/biography are forms of empirical narrative where linearity dominates. Anita Desai partially rejects such a mode; she follows instead, a mode which is existentialist, surrialist, and which is able to fathom a character in all his/her bewildering variety and nuances. Anita Desai believes in creating those characters who resist the flow of narrative.

Dr. N. Raj Gopal thoroughly analyses all the novels of Anita Desai from the stylistic point of views. The value of the book is inhanced by the chapter on technique in Anita Desai's novels. Dr. N. Raj Gopal examines the introvert, and hyper-sensitive Maya, the lonely Monisha, the rebel Nirode, a frustrated Sita, a discarded Nanda, characteristic Raka, Bim, Deven, Sarah and Adit and others. All these characters live at different levels of reality, consume it, and reproduce it in a manner that remains solitary, alienated and contextually self-breeding. Dr. Gopal excels in probing the character stage by stage referring to available scholarship and text in question. This formal method is highly acceptable and even desirable. Dr. Gopal Rao also comments on the multiple points of view adopted by Anita Desai, syntax of her sentence, lyricism in her novels, an so on, presenting, finally, her total vision of life and man. I am sure this study will go a long way not only in initiating the uninitiated to the novels of Anita Desai; it will also inspire the professional scholar to study the psychological aspects of her novels more rigorously and theoretically than studied so far. Dr. Gopal contributes vitally to the available literature on Anita Desai.

CHARU SHEEL SINGH

PREFACE

Anita Desai (1937 —) is a very distinguished Indian English novelist and has been recognised as such both in India and abroad. She has written in, and experimented with, varieties of the genres of fiction like the short story, the literature for children and review articles and interviews which carry their own fictional interest and flavour. The recognition of the depth and variety in Anita Desai's novels is testified by the fact that scholarship has been continuously growing upon her work.[1]

The available scholarship notwithstanding, there is a great deal of scope to work on the technical aspect of Anita Desai's novels. This study makes a modest attempt to focus attention upon technique as it relates itself to the themes in the novels of Anita Desai. My effort has been to analyse the themes of her different novels under certain major titles and devote the last chapter exclusively to Anita Desai's fictional technique. There are several book-length studies about her work as given in the Bibliography but there is hardly any exclusive study devoted to her fictional technique. Most of the critics have not said much about this important aspect of her novels. The justification for undertaking this study is the woeful lack of critical material on her fictional technique. My approach has been, for the most part, analytical and integrationist in terms of the total life perspective presented in Anita Desai's novels.

The first chapter "Introduction" discusses some important aspects of fictional technique in general, quoting extensively from different critics on the subject. The chapter also deals with some major themes of Anita Desai's novels and throws light on her technical skill.

---

1. Anita Desai's Popularity can be guaged by the fact that one of her novels (*In Custody*) is already filmed.

The second chapter ''Feminine Psyche'' deals with different aspects of feminine psyche which constitute a major part of her fictional material. The novels have been selected from the point of view of female characters, such characters who represent different aspects of feminine psyche. These characters cover a wide range of age-groups, and have different personalities and characteristics some of which are neurotic and sub-normal.

The third chapter ''Familial Relationships'' deals with the novels which focus on family. Different varieties of familial relationships have been discussed here. Relationships are not necessarily pleasant and the tension in familial relationship is obvious.

The fourth chapter entitled ''As A Social Being'' discusses the novels that deal with the characters in relation to society. Man is a social animal and therefore howsoever individualistic he may be, he cannot be seen in isolation from society. Society as a shaping and controlling influence on the individual is the focus of this chapter.

The fifth and the last chapter ''Anita Desai's Fictional Technique'' deals with various technical devices that she has used in her novels.The technical devices take stock of her use of symbolism, imagery, dialogue, language, narrative technique, etc.

The book ends with a ''Conclusion'' which is an enumeration of inferences reached at after making the study. Anita Desai may not be a technical innovator but she is a skilled writer using techniques which contribute to effective story telling.

We may agree or disagree with the propriety of her using quotes from poems to pinpoint the mood of the situation but it is certain that it is a device used frequently by her.

The relevant existing criticism on different novels has been discussed when the novels are analysed in the book. Sometimes there are repetitions of textual quotations in the body of the book, but doing so becomes unavoidable because the same novel has been discussed under different themes which provide scheme for chapter division. My indebtedness to existing criticism has been acknowledged in the body of the thesis and also in Bibliography.

I have received valuable support, encouragement and supervision from the following : Prof. R.P. Singh, Head, Department of English, Kashi Vidyapith, Dr. Suman Kumar, Reader, Department of English, Kashi Vidyapith, Dr. P.K. Pandey, Department of English, Banaras Hindu University, all the above distinguished scholars are specially thanked for their labour in shaping me and my work. Special thanks are due to Dr. Charu Sheel Singh, Reader, Department of English, Kashi Vidyapith for giving valuable suggestions for final preparation of the manuscript before publication.

My borhters Shri N. Ram Krishna, Deputy Commondant, N. Venket Narsimha, Srinivas Ramanuj and their wives N. Lakshmi and N. Sharda have been a source of encouragement during the study.

I must not forget to express my gratitude to my respected father and mother who are responsible for whatever modest achievement including the present study I could have in my life.

The book is brought out in hope that it will prove helpful for students and teachers alike.I take this opportunity to thank to Dr. K.R. Gupta of the M/s Atlantic Publishers and Distributors for professionally publishing this book.

VARANASI **N. RAJ GOPAL**

CONTENTS

Chapter I

INTRODUCTION

The Indo-Anglian Fiction presents a consistent picture of the changing social realities during this eventful century. Those interested in categorising may find it convenient to divide the Indian English fiction into two broad categories, *viz.* the pre-and post-Independence groups of writers. While the pioneers like M.R. Anand, R.K. Narayan, Raja Rao and also Bhabani Bhattacharya depict the socio-economic and political realities of Indian life, their successors of the more recent times find it difficult to use the powerful medium of the novel for just light-hearted dilly-dallying. They too appear as much concerned with a new variety of challenges and problems as their worthy predecessors had been with the gross realities of caste and class conflicts, exploitation, and the proverbial Indian poverty. The fact is that centuries of slavery and oppression had made India a problematical country and the fact of Independence while highlighting these ills also made Indians conscious of the necessity of removing them.

What Paul Vergies in his perceptive study of the problems of Indian English fiction writers found as their stock material is now a little bit outdated in the sense that the more recent Indian writers of fiction in English are extending their ken to explore the psychological and sociological strains in the social and individual life. Joan Rockwell in her study of fiction deals with the crucial relationship between fiction and life and tells that whenever historic moments occur in the life of a nation the period round that moment sees intense fictional activity. She calls such moments "nodal periods". The post-Independence period in the recent Indian history corresponds suitably with her concept of the "nodal period" when a number of Indian writers of fiction in English try to explore and manifest Indian reality. In these writers we do not find either the commitment of the earlier period or even the amused narration of the trials of the middle class, trying to unite the past traditional outlook with the fast emerging realities of the modern living conditions. In this effort the writers of the post-Independence phase move inward. They get more and more psychologically intended and try to assess the sociological effect on the psyche of their characters.

Fortunately this movement from the outward gross realities to inward complexities found as its mouth-piece a number of women novelists who by the peculiar situation of their existence have been able to see the Indian complexities from close quarters, where constraints of varied hues and shades work upon the sensitive individuals. Of these women novelists, Anita Desai happens to be the leading voice. We may miss in her fiction the customary strains of rural poverty, caste and class conflict, but she has fascinating stories to tell about individuals who have to traverse a ground too tricky and treacherous to handle smoothly.

She becomes therefore a recorder of the dilemma faced by an individual in the Indian urban set-up. She gets interested in analysis and portrayal of human relationship. The novel is essentially a vehicle for delineating human relationships mostly baffling in nature in the sense that man's actions and volitions often take to uncertain ways under different situations. We notice that among women novelists at least Anita Desai and Kamala Markandeya do not make human relationships only of peripheral interest, rather they make them central to their main fictional concern. Since human relationships tell upon the mental and emotional springs, they very often tend to be complicated out of which a talented creative artist can weave gripping story-patterns. In such situations the emotional idealism and practical realities are also very often at variance. Such was the case with Prince Hamlet and such are the stories of Anita Desai. The innermost psyche of her protagonists is revealed to us through their interaction with those who are emotionally related to them on the basis of kinship. For the purposes of fiction no human relationship is more fertile and potential than that in the family and specially among the kins. Desai knows this crucial fact and that is why her novels depict such relationships as they are based on emotional idealism. She is not an idealist; she is simply a recorder of the situations, but the emotional crises among kins are born of the realisation that the kins fall short of the ideal in such relationships. This fact is substantiated by almost all of her novels. Anita's *Cry the Peacock* is concerned with the dissonance and disharmony that disrupts the marital relationship between Maya and Gautam. The *Voices in the City* depicts the disintegration of Nirode's, Monisha's and Amla's lives caused by imbalances in familial ties. *Bye-Bye Black Bird* shreds to pieces the hypothesis that East and West can never meet to form lasting equations. Sarah and Adit care for each other's happiness even at the cost of being marginalised and condemned to live in two societies and in two, not merely different, but antagonistic cultures. *Where Shall We Go This Summer ?* emphasises the universal need for human ties with Sita awakening to the fact that even sky and earth try to meet each other near the horizon. The *Fire on the Mountain* conveys the message that running away from human contacts or one's kin is not a desirable proposition. Thus the above references indicate the nature and the thematic thrust of Desai's novels.

In order to place Anita Desai in proper perspective it is necessary to see her along with the other women novelists who have more or less the same thematic concern and who in their own way deal with the commonly shared theme of human relationship. All of them are chroniclers of the tension in the wake of India's emergence as a developing nation. For a better and easier understanding of this aspect of modern Indian women fiction writers in English we may look for general tendencies which unmistakably point towards certain commonly shared themes in their fiction.

One of the themes recurring in the novels written during the post-Independence decades is the individual's nostalgia in treating the joint family. Often the central figures in the novels, in order to seek their own identities consciously, try to break away from the kind of life they are nostalgic for. The institution of the joint-family gives opportunity for group human behaviour, it symbolises an expansive pre-industrial way of life; and it represents a deeply entrenched form of orthodoxy against which the individual may find himself helpless. It gives way to presenting the conflict between two sets of values — one standing for the supremacy of social hierarchy and the other for that of the individual.

The treatment of the theme by women novelists is a three-faceted affair. A personal story slowly develops into a wider conflict in which are involved the individual's identity for supremacy and the social demands. The personal story thus is used as a springboard to explore social change in India in all its complex manifestations. They seem to examine the transition from a traditional society to an urban industrial metropolitan society in its comprehensiveness.

The comparative achievement of Anita Desai becomes clear when we notice that her fellow women writers like Kamala Markandeya, Ruth Jhabwala, Nayantara Sehgal, Shanta Ramarao and Atiya Hussain seldom try to portray the psychic elements involved in these themes in their fullness. The tensions and anxieties of being modern in a traditional society have been overlooked by most of these writers who have mainly devoted their attention to broad social features that emerge in the course of gradual metamorphosis of the old order. So intense is their devotion to the physical aspects of this change that they fail to take note of and project the psychological reality which must, of necessity, be allowed an upper hand in the face of the world undergoing a rapid change with the advancement of scientific and technological knowledge and rapid progress of communication and industrialisation.

Anita Desai adds a new dimension to English fiction by concentrating on the exploration of this troubled sensibility a typical modern Indian phenomenon. In contrast to her in Jhabwala's work the social background is rather more important than the characters, in Kamala Markandeya's works the emphasis is as much on the principal characters as on matters — economic, political, social and cultural. Nayantara Sehgal while dealing with social problems, confines herself to a particular social class, namely the upper class and the aristocracy.

Anita Desai thus clearly stands ahead the group in as much as she introduces a shift of ideational focus from the outer to the inner part of human existence. Her novels focus on the inner climate, the climate of sensibility. Her main concern is to depict the psychic states of her protagonists at some crucial juncture of their lives. To sustain her effort she has forged a style supple and suggestive enough, to convey the fever and fretfulness, to record the eddies and currents in the stream of consciousness of her characters. The inter play of thoughts, feelings and emotions is reflected in language, syntax and imagery.

Anita's achievement would appear sufficiently significant if we remain mindful of her problems of devising the proper metaphor to express the workings of the inner mind. Though she has had the model of the Brontes, she had few Indian models to follow and thus it is on her own that she succeeds in evolving a technique and suitable style to communicate the critical ordeal in which the individual is placed in her novels.

Anita Desai thus tries to introduce a modern psychological vein and projects a sensibility generally not encountered in other Indo-Anglian writers of fiction. As a novelist her distinguishing qualities are many, the chief among them being the subordination of the background to the characters and the deft handling of language, imagery and syntax in order to convey an intimate expression of the inner world of her characters. She insists on analysing her characters and the story is important only in so far as it reflects the obsessions of her characters. Free from the journalistic enthusiasm for depicting the socio-political life in India, Mrs. Desai makes each work of hers a haunting exploration of the psychic self. The work is executed so thoroughly that her treatment gets the look of a philosophical system — a system which has been familiar to the world in the form of "Existentialism". It may be recalled that in the 50s and 60s Existentialist philosophy had become quite fashionable among the progressive urban intellectuals. Mrs. Desai finds its theories suitable to her themes. Aspects of Existentialism are in evidence in the total framework of her stories. Its emphasis on the alienation of man from an 'absurd' world, his consequent estrangement from "normal" society, and his recognition of the world as negative and meaningless — presents the sensitive individual, fragmented and spiritually destroyed by the particular social conditions of life, a life complex enough to make him obsessed. This particular phase of existentialism — "the one alone," the man who has no record, — seems to be a favourite subject of Desai. Loneliness is not something unique, but is, in fact, a characteristic of the society of our time. Today, many individuals feel alone, unrelated to others, unable to communicate with those around them, unable to feel at one with them. This problem of an individual who feels emotionally and spiritually alone forms the backbone of Desai's themes. The inner yearning of the lonely one for understanding and affection — a recurrent theme in poetry and fiction — occurs here also. The moving description of loneliness leaves a lasting impression on the reader's mind: Maya, Nirode, Amla, Monisha, Sarah, Sita, Nanda Kaul — all suffer from a sense of isolation that is not merely physical but also psychic. What is more, their respective personality traits and attitudes also determine the mental and emotional effect on their isolation. This estrangement from which they suffer is, in fact, the consequence of the absence of desired relationships rather than the absence of contacts, the lack is not of company but of companionship. They find themselves alone and anxious in a world in which they are unable to establish emotionally satisfying social affinities. Characters like Maya and Sita are isolated — first by their own inability "to see things steadily and see them whole" which disrupts their relationship with others, and secondly, by the tendency of others to withdraw from them and treat them as if they were in some way a different and frightful kind of beings. Bewildered by a world which they do not understand and which does not understand them, they feel tragically and pathetically alone. In their retreat from reality, they cut themselves off from communication with the rest of the world. And ironically the retreat begun by such "mentally ill" characters, in an effort to escape from situations of intolerable loneliness, ends as in the case of Maya, in a state of utter isolation far more fearsome. Through her cry there reverberates the anguish of acute loneliness.

> "I am in a fever, stop me! Silence me! Or I will fly on; fly up, at you, through you, past you, and away. For I am ill. I am in a fever, God, in a fever." (181)[1]

The leading thematic motif of loneliness is brought home to us by a conscious effort on the part of the novelist to describe the contributory factors to it. Mrs. Desai lays much stress on them so much so that sometimes a certain contributory factor looks like the theme itself. For example : we notice an elaborate description of the break-down of channels of communication between husband and wife. This snapping of communication link is mainly by the incompatibility of temperament between the two. And this phenomenon of dissimilarity in attitudes, resulting in unsatisfactory relationships, runs through all the six novels.

With her early childhood nurtured in the world of Brontes she has imbibed depth and hue of the fiction-writers of the West. At the age of nine she had read *Wuthering Heights.* Ever since, literature interested her most. In her twenties she read the novels of Lawrence, Woolf, James and Proust which exerted deep influence on her. More recently, she read Kawabata and more and more modern poetry — particularly that of Rimbaud, Hopkins, and Lawrence — which deeply influenced her novels. These western novelists and poets suited her purpose and she makes, like them, the use of flash-backs and stream of consciousness techniques in some of her novels. If the western writers presented her with general criteria for her choicest field, the poets of the East furnished her with the charm of rhythms and style. Whatever she heartily welcomed was deeply and successfully entrenched within to enrich her creative perspectives. Even a cursory glance at her works would reveal three important

1. Anita Desai: *Cry the Peacock* (Delhi: Orient Paperbacks, 1980), p. 181.

areas of excellence: characterisation, theme and plot structure. The three attain their desired thrust because of her style, unique in its own way, which is beautifully suited to her need and the characters and themes are neatly organised under a compact pattern so that each novel becomes as it were, a distinctive world in miniature.

Characters in the novels of Mrs. Desai are generally neurotic females, highly sensitive but sequestered in a world of dream and imagination and alienated from their surroundings as a consequence of their failure or unwillingness to adjust with the reality. They often differ in their opinion from others and embark on a long voyage of contemplation in order to find the meaning of their existence. Having wandered for long, they usually arrive at a juncture where either they find that after all their urgency has been in some essential manner very significant as in the case of Bim in *Clear Light of Day* or sometimes simply damage themselves, unable to solve the mystery that envelops their suffering, like Maya and Monisha. Her characters build a large spectrum. There are individuals of multifarious dimensions, like the detached and practical Gautam, the rebel Nirode; the artist Dharma, the sensitive immigrant Dev and others.

Coming to her themes, Anita Desai seems to have opted for portraying various themes at a time in her novels and in each individual novel these themes seem to be occurring again and again. She usually starts by presenting persons who are cut out in different grains from others. They resist the demand of society and turn out to be rebels. Not finding a proper channel of communication they become alienated and start brooding on their lives. All their wanderings and reflections finally bring them into new vistas of understanding which they had formerly ignored or rejected. Anita Desai's themes are thus original and entirely different from those of Indo-Anglian novelists. Her novels are not political or sociological in character but are engaged in exposing the labyrinths of the human mind and in indicating the ways to psychological fulfilment. Thus, her themes tend to wedge off the tracks of other novelists. Each aspect merges with the other and sometimes one finds a number of themes woven together. Using these themes as a foundation the writer is able to build up her characters into a significant whole.

A writer dealing with the psychological aspects of characters has to employ a certain design by which the inner working of the protagonist's mind is unfolded to the readers gradually with the progress of the narrative. As in the case of her themes and her characters Anita Desai's plots too are not repetitive. Each book has an individual structural pattern of its own. However, all the mechanisms she employs lend the work a unique harmony where incidents, people, situation combine to produce an artistic whole.

One can say that Anita Desai's plots are not so much deliberate contrivances as natural and inevitable outgrowth of the theme and perspective. As the story advances she seems to be quietly sliding in her scenes, settings and characters, without much of an advance preparation. As her forte is the psychic presentation of individual human beings, the narrative is rightly allowed to move freely and not clogged by blocks and patterns artificially imposed from outside. But it is not as if there is no subtlety or control in plot structure. The plot is always simple and neat enough so as not to impede the psychological revelation, and it is always well defined enough to present her vision clearly. Her plot structure, therefore, shows a splendid fusion of form and expression, contrivance and spontaneity.

Regarding structural part of her fiction it is only proper to quote the novelist herslef:

> "I start writing without having very much of a 'Plot' in my mind or on paper — only a very hazy idea of what the pattern of the book is to be. But it seems to work itself out as I go along, quite naturally and inevitably. I prefer the word 'Pattern' to 'Plot' as it sounds more natural — and even better, if I dare use it, is Hopkins' word 'inscape' — while 'plot' sounds arbitrary, heavy-headed and artificial — all that I wish to avoid. One should have a pattern and then fit each piece in keeping with the others and so forming a balanced whole."[2]

After all a writer's aim is not merely to tell a story, to amuse us or move us, but to force us to think, to understand the hidden meaning of events. In Anita Desai's novels, life is depicted as it really is — life, as rule of the upper middle class which she knows very well and which she can treat sympathetically. She doesn't draw upon second-hand information for the ground-work of her plots. Rather by seeing life itself and depicting it in her stories exactly as she views it, she gives to her work an authenticity and a validity of its own. This ample knowledge of life is obtained through direct observation and insight. Her carefully pondered observations help to make her treatment of

2. Atma Ram Sharma, "An Interview with Anita Desai," *World Literature Written in English*, Vol. 16, No. 1, April 1977, p. 101.

the events, actions, and men more realistic. The profound sensation of truth she effects, is provided through artful and expert transitions and by dexterity of the composition. Dostoevsky too says — "to write a novel there must be one or more strong impressions that the author has really experienced to the depth of his being."[3] Anita Desai herself states in an interview,

> "In countless, small ways scenes and settings certainly belong to my life. Many of the minor characters and incidents are also based on real life. But the major characters and the major events are either entirely imaginary or an amalgamation of several characters and happenings. One can use the raw material of life only very selectively. It is common among writers to pick out something from real life and develop their situations around that while there are others who start from some real experience, which continuously grows in their imagination. You use it as a base but don't confine yourself to it."[4]

The story is an account of certain people in a given situation. Since the novelist's subject is man in society, his subject matter must also be the texture of manners and conventions by which a social being defines his own identity. In the sphere of Indo-Anglian writing one finds that many great writers have been much concerned with depicting real life. Realism, in one form or the other, had always been used in Hindu texts like the Puranas, the Mahabharata, the Ramayana, etc. The fact is that "the art novel in India found its cradle in realism."[5] The earliest Indian novels written in Bengali, consisted of sketches of contemporary Bengali society. Social realism was depicted in the twenties by various writers like Sharat Chandra Chatterjee and Munshi Prem Chand who wrote in Bengali, Hindi and Urdu respectively. Since then Indian writers in English have shown interest in contemporary social and political issues.

Anita Desai in an interview with Yashodhara Dalmia, says —

> "Most things are so very ethereal .... They pass and they change so very quickly. To make a report on some general events is not

---

3. The *Writer's Creative Individuality and the Development of Literature*, Moscow:, Express Publishers, 1977, p. 76.

4. Anita Desai, "In an Interview with Yashodhara Dalmia," *The Times of India*, April 29, 1979.

5. Hari Mohan Prasad, "Dimensions of Realism in "Indo-Anglian Fiction", *The Indian Journal of English Studies*, Vol. XXI, 1981-82, p. 131.

of so much importance. There are other elements which remain basic to our lives. I mean the human condition itself. It is only superficially affected by the day-to-day changes. We continue to live in the same way as we have in the past centuries ... with the same tragedies and the same comedies. And that is why it interests me."[6]

In Desai's stories action is subordinated to psychology. The central themes revolve around the mental and spiritual developments of the dramatis personae and not on their physical adventures. This relegation of action to a secondary place enables us to understand more profoundly the how and why of a situation. In this respect the writer shows a close affinity with Virginia Woolf who also entered the consciousness of the characters and showed little concern for the actual outside action. The theme of Desai's novels like that of the novels of James Joyce and Virginia Woolf, is human nature and human relationships. Her stories are peopled with men and women such as we see around us and with happenings such as might occur any day to such people. The central theme of man-woman relationship with which Desai deals has been treated by several other Indian writers like Nayantara Sehgal, Nargis Dalal, and Kamala Das. But in Desai the themes are governed by existential tones. The existential perspective on the theme of individual and society is evident in all the stories. By way of definition, it may be said that the main themes dealt with by the existential thinkers are those of alienation, despair, frustration, anxiety and the emotional life of the individuals. In the words of F.H. Heinemann, "The problem of existentialism is in a narrower sense expressive of the present crisis of man, and in a broader sense, of the enduring human condition."[7] Modern thinkers speak more readily of 'human condition' than of human nature. By condition, they mean, more or less definitely; the limits which outline man's fundamental situation in the universe. And in this respect, Desai is essentially an existentialist novelist as she is seriously concerned with this "human condition," and also shows profound skill in exploring the "emotional life" of the people in the stories.

In the light of her above observation we can easily understand Desai's 'patterns' and also her relationship with the main currents of the English novel.

---

6. Anita Desai, "In an Interview with Yashodhara Dalmia," *The Times of India*, April 29, 1979.

7. *Existentialism and the Modern Predicament*, London, Admn. and Charles Black, 1953, p. 178.

No study of thematic pattern alone can be useful unless we pay attention to the structural components of a work of art. Almost all the major critics on the form of fiction have underlined the correlation between theme and structure. Instead of being detained by this complex problem we may just note a few telling comnents on this aspect. Devid Cecil has observed that the novel —

> "... should have the formal qualities common to all good works of art, unity, pattern, harmony. But it must also seem probable in the sense that other fiction need not; it must give an illusion of life as it is or has been lived in the actual world. To achieve both these objects at the same time is hard. Read life, as we know it, is not distinguished by unity, pattern and harmony. On the contrary, it is a heterogeneous, disorderly, indeterminate affair full of loose ends and false starts and irrelevant details. How is the novelist to reconcile these two claims, how keep the delicate balance between the demands of life and art? This is his central, special problem as a craftsman."[8]

According to him an awareness of this problem helps a critic to judge the novel's worth.

It is evident, therefore, that any novel howsoever faithful in recording the impressions of the novelist and in satisfying our sense of curiosity about life, will be artistically unsatisfactory if it is merely a concatenation of incidents and episodes. It can hardly be accepted as an artistic piece of creation, unless a sense of equilibrium and design is imparted to the arrangement of the impressions. In its absence the novelist can scarcely manage to satisfy our curiosity of life. Hence any work of consequence should meet these conditions; Walter Allen is emphatic that "if the novelist can do both, we are entitled to say he is greater — other things being equal — than one who does not."[9]

Every art-form is governed by its specific laws, but there are certain general principles which apply to all. Of them the most fundamental is the principle of harmony between form and content, or in technical terms, between the theme and the structure of a work of art. The greater the degree of harmony, the greater will be the

---

8. As quoted by John Colmer, *Approaches to the Novels*, London, Oliver and Boyd, 1967, p. 5.
9. Essay on Trollope contained in Portraits, as quoted by Walter Allen in *The English Novel*, Pelican Book, 1965, p. 18.

intensity of its appeal. The novel too, should be true to this principle. Its greatness as an artistic creation can be judged by determining the extent to which its theme and the resultant structure are inevitable and interdependent.

The whole confused mass of material presented by the novelist falls into some sequence, spatial, or temporal, and submits itself to a particular design, descriptive, dramatic or pictorial, and thus as we turn the pages of the novel one after another, "the impressions that succeed one another... are built into a structure."[10] It is obvious that it is owing to this definite arrangement and organisation of the novelist's material that we get a complete and coherent view of life observed from a particular angle The finished work, thus, is the outcome of the two forces working simultaneously upon the mass of material which the novelist has chosen for his treatment, namely, the shaping pressure of his personal vision of the world (which manifests itself as the subject or the theme of the novel), and the aesthetic sensibility of the novelist which imparts an appropriate and abstract beauty of form to the novel and impels him to fuse every element into vital relationship. To be brief "... Every novel is an extended metaphor of the author's view of life." This is how Sir Walter Allen establishes the relationship between the novel and the novelist. It is so, in his opinion, because "every novelist... gives us in his novels his own personal idiosyncratic vision of the world."[11]

Henry James. too said the same thing when he defined the novels as "a personal impression of life."[12] While the novelist sets himself to the arrangement and organisation of his impressions and tries to impart a design to the novel, he focuses his attention on some central idea, which makes everything converge on one point. This central idea, which may be precisely called the "theme" of the novel, is the unifying and controlling factor in the organisation of his material. Flaubert called this central idea or the theme of the novel "the mother idea," and was of the view that this was the governing factor from which "all the rest flow in the novel."[13]

10. Percy Lubbock, The Craft of Fiction, Walter Allen in *The English Novel*, London, Jonathan Cape, Pelican Book, 1965, p. 19.

11. Walter Allen, *Ibid.*, 17.

12. Henry James, "The Art of Fiction", *American Literature of 19th Century: An Anthology*, India, Eurasia Publishing House, 1965, p. 508.

13. Flaubert, Correspondence, as cited by Robert Ciddel in *A Treatise on the Novel*, London, Jonathan Cape, 1960, p 37.

It is obvious that the theme is the very nucleus of the whole design. All the components of the novel *viz.* plot, characterisation, description and setting, the narrative method and style are subject to its shaping pressure. They are balanced and functionally related to each other to create a real unity under the magnetic field of the theme. The plot structure gets deformed, characters "get out of hand" or "run away" (to borrow Forster's expression), descriptions become out of place and verbose, incidents and events become irrelevant and improbable, the choice of narrative design becomes unsuitable, if the theme ceases to exercise its restraints. It is thus an all-pervading essence embracing the entire length of the novel.

From the above discussion it appears that an anatomical study of the novel reveals that it is a complex but harmonious fusion of the different limbs of the novels under the pressure of the theme. The unity we observe in the whole design of the novel is achieved because the novel in its final shape is a natural growth at author's attempt to evolve and realise his proposed theme. The form of the novel may be called "structure." By "structure" we mean, a living form which the novel assumes during the exposition of the theme, and which is "single, integral, and organic." This idea of the organic structure which is true of any work of art, has been defined by Herbert Read in his introductory essay in the *Collected Essays* where he says:

> "When a work of art has its own inherent laws, originating with its very invention and fusing in one vital unity both structure and content, then the resulting form may be described as organic."[14]

Thus this principle of "vital unity" between "form" and "content" may be taken as a yardstick to measure the artistic worth of any work of art. The degree of their organic integration determines the degree of its artistic success. The theme remains absolutely an abstract hypothesis, until it is realised and developed through the various limbs of the novel. The point is made clear by the writers of the book *Understanding Fiction* in their observations :

> "He (the novelist) knows that, when he sets out to write a story, he is really engaged in a process of exploration and experiment: he is exploring the nature of his characters and the meaning of their acts, and, too he is exploring his own feelings about them.

---

14. Herbert Read, *Collected Essays in Criticism*, London, Faber and Faber Ltd., 1950, p. 19.

He knows that any shift in the organisation of his story, or any variation in style, will alter, however slightly, the total response."[15]

Style or technique of delivering the thematic thrust, thus is the vital agent through which the theme becomes a harmonious pattern. In fact of the six components of novel given above. The proverbial "Style is the man" has been happily modified by Mark Schorer : "one should correct Buffon and say the style is the subject".[16] Obviously, in his opinion, in the choice of the style, the author must be conditioned by the demands of his subject.

Style is "the life-blood" of the idea, but the idea remains an abstraction till it is realised through language. Hence language is the main element of style. Being so, it is essential, therefore, that the language must be a matter of deep consideration for the novelist. He should always be conscious of the fact that it is by the proper use of language alone that he can give proper expression to his idea. According to Anthony Trollope:

> "It is not sufficient that there be a meaning which may be hammered out of the sentence, but that the language should be so pellucid that the meaning should be rendered without an effort to the reader; — and not only some proportion of the meaning, but the very sense, no more and no less, which the writer has intended to put into his words."[17]

Maupassant, also, one of the chief masters of style laid great emphasis on the exactness of style. In his opinion it can be achieved only through the selection of exact words. He observed: "Whatever you want to say, there is one word to express it, one verb to set it in motion and only one adjective to describe it. And so you must hunt for this word, this verb and this adjective until you find them." He maintained that it is possible to convey and demonstrate the most subtle notions by following the dictum of Boileau that 'A word in its place is a symbol of strength.' He further pointed out that to catch various shades of thought it is not necessary that the novelist should choose "eccentric vocabulary, complicated, elaborate and exotic." "... it is necessary to distinguish with extreme clarity all the shifts in

---

15. Cleanth Brooks, Jr. and Robert Penn Warren, *Understanding Fiction,* New York, Appleton Century — Crofts, Inc., 1948, p. 570.

16. Phillip Freund, *The Art of Reading Novels*, New York, Collier Books, 1966, p. 233.

17. As quoted by Miriam Allott in *Novelists on the Novel,* London, Routledge and Kegan Paul, 1959, p. 315.

value which a word undergoes according to the place it occupies ... Let us try to make ourselves excellent stylists rather than collectors of uncommon terms,'' he suggested.

The ''pellucid'' language and the exactness of words, the two essential requisites of style which are mentioned above, can be easily obtained only if the novelist is conscious of his theme.

The use of dialogues is one of the features of the artistically conceived novels. Dialogues, well managed, become one of the most delightful stylistic devices, through which the author enables the reader to get into touch with his characters most intimately. Using it, the narrative approaches the vividness and naturalness of drama. Besides brightening a narrative, good dialogues when used judiciously, serve many technical purposes.

Though the dialogue is frequently employed in the evolution of plot — its principal function is connected with the exposition of character.

Any discussion of the structure of the novel would be incomplete unless the points of view of the author are taken into consideration; for this is the organising principle which knits up every thread of the novel, to make it a sustained single image. A close examination of the point of view of the author, as the novel gradually develops under the pressure of the theme, gives one the idea of its structure.

When the narrative scheme is critically analysed, we can see how the author has harmonised the different limbs of the novel. The novelist does not always treat his character, or narrate his story from a particular point of view throughout. According to the demand of the occasion he shifts his point of view. Hence, in his narrative scheme, he is by turns omniscient and ignorant, direct and oblique, a dramatist and the teller of tales.

Percy Lubbock has illustrated this through Flaubert's viewpoint in *Madam Bovary* :

> Flaubert handles his materials quite differently from point to point. Sometimes he seems to be describing what he has seen himself ... his object is to place the scene before us, so that we may take it in like a picture gradually unrolled or a drama enacted. But again the method changes. There comes a juncture at which for some reason, it is necessary for us to know more than we could have made out by simply looking and listening, Flaubert, the author of the story, must intervene with his

> superior knowledge... or it may be that he who naturally knows everything, even the inmost, unexpected thought of the characters, — wishes us to share, the mind of Bovary, of Emma, not to wait only on their words and actions, and so he goes below the surface and enters their consciousness, and describes the train of sentiment that passes there...[18]

It is obvious from this analysis that "a very 'impersonal' writer like Flaubert, too, cannot stick to one point of view; he has to make use of many. And this is true of every novelist. He should be conscious of the varying demands of the novel and should select the suitable point of view accordingly. They are "few and simple but infinite in their possibilities of fusion and combination." They can be arranged into a new design to suit every new theme that the writer takes in hand.

Thus we can assess the quality of the structure of a novel by studying the mangement of the different points of view of the author. For example in Conrad's *Lord Jim* the story develops through various characters. A study of Conrad's management of the points of view yields many traits of the structure of this novel. So also in *Wuthering Heights*, according to Andrew H. Wright:

> Great complexity of point of view is achieved by reason of the fact that there are several layers of narrations between the reader and the events.[19]

The above discussion has aimed at showing how theme and various components of the novel, which constitute the total structure, are interdependent. In the words of S. Kumar "when a novelist combines and fuses all these units harmoniously and organically, the outcome is a fine work of art. On the contrary, any disparity between them renders the whole work a lopsided product."[20]

Lubbock's famous remark makes as good a comment as one could wish for on this point:

> The best form is that which makes the most of its subject — there is no other definition of form in fiction. The well-made book is that in which the subject and the form coincide and are

---

18. Percy Lubbock, *Ibid.*, pp. 64-65.

19. Andrew H. Wright, *Jane Austen's Novels: A Study in Structure*, p. 64.

20. S. Kumar, *The Fictional Art of Somerset Maugham*, Varanasi, Kashividyapeeth Publications, 1977, pp. 56-57.

> indistinguishable — book in which the matter is all used up in the form, in which the form expresses all the matter. Where there is disagreement and conflict between the two, there is stuff that is wanting; the form of the book, as it stands before us, has failed to do justice to the idea.[21]

We have seen that structure is not superimposed — a mere external trapping, but an inevitable formal manipulation of the "mother idea." The successful work of art is that in which the theme finds its perfect flowering in the structure, for according to Henry James, perfect execution demands a full integration of the idea with its mode of expression, so that we may lose our sense of the story being a blade drawn out of its sheath. He succinctly remarks : "... the idea and form, are needle and thread" and neither can have any use without the other.[22]

Anita Desai has tried to present her themes organically with appropriate adjustment and adaptations in spheres of style and point of view. The result is her comparative superiority over other Indian women novelists writing in English. By deft management of the form she succeeds in attaining the proper form on which Lubbock is so insistent. After having discussed the basics of Anita Desai's fictional methods we are now equipped to analyse her novels in detail so as to discover how she attains remarkable success as a novelist.

---

21. Percy Lubbock, *Ibid.*, p. 40.

22. Henry James, " The Art of Fiction," *American Literature of the Nineteenth Century : An Anthology*, Eds. Fisher, Reninger *et al*, New Delhi, Eurasia Publishing House Ltd., 1990, p. 517.

Chapter II

FEMININE PSYCHE

The rise of Feminism as a movement on the continent began with the crucial question that portrayal of women by male aritsts must be deficient for, even the most imaginative of male writers is by no means equipped to give an authentic rendering of the female sensibility. Of late there has been a tendency among the women Indian novelists writing in English to share this view. There has emerged a group of women novelists who try to give their own side of the story from their own point of view.

Women have always been the subject of literary work but literature has mostly been created by men. A genuine question that arises is how much men know about the feminine psyche. And even if they know much or little how for is it true? Psychologists too believe that the male carries some rudiments of the female. Medical science informs us that there is no gender difference in the beginning. It is only later that they assume gender characteristics. But more important are the psychic characteristics.

Women writers of all ages have a natural preference for writing about women characters. Such preference may be a limitation to their creativity, as in case of Jane Austen who excels in her two inches of ivory. But this limitation does not in any way reduce the importance of women writers. Anita Desai is no exception insofar as she has written by and large about women characters and no wonder if most of her novels move around women characters. Although she is pre-occupied with the theme of incompatible marital couples yet we come across different kinds of women characters in her novels. Because of her preoccupation with women characters many studies have come out on the subject. Many critics have addressed themselves to the theme of broken marriage and ill-matched couples in her novels but this doesn't mean that her exploration of feminine psyche ends here. Besides the hypersensitive types verging on neuroticism, we also have several other kinds. Such characters may be minor ones in her novels but they represent woman's mind and psyche in it varied moods and nuances.

If at one extreme there are sensitive women characters, on the other extreme, we also find thick-skinned women with blunt sensibility. In her very first novel *Cry the Peacock* we find examples of the two extremes.

Cry the Peacock, is a novel mainly concerned with the theme of disharmony between husband and wife relationship. Here Anita Desai has dealt with a sterile woman, highly sensitive and emotional, who is married to Gautama, a promising, prosperous and overbusy practitioner of law. Gautama's sensibilities are too rough and practical to suit Maya's. She is the pampered child of a Rai Saheb, and is brought up in an atmosphere of luxury. She lives, to use her own words, like "a toy prince in a toy world". Though Gautama is a faithful husband who takes care of Maya and loves her in his own way yet Maya is never satisfied and happy. She feels that Gautama never cares for her and does not have any feelings for her. The novel gives us an impression of the marital incompatibility and unhappy conjugal life. The novel begins with the death of Maya's pet dog Toto. This makes matter worse. This event upsets Maya so terribly that she is off her mental balance. Being childless she is much attached to the dog and it seems that the dog was a child substitute:

> "Childless women do develop fanatic attachments to their pets, they say. It is no less a relationship than that of a woman and her child, no less worthy of reverence, and agonised remembrance."[1]

But Gautama a practical man takes this event easy and makes arrangement for its burial, consoles Maya in his own way and says that he would bring another dog for her. His indifference hurts Maya. Toto's death may be trivial for Gautama, a rational and professionally busy man, but it matters a lot to Maya. We get scores of such examples throughout the novel where Gautama neglects emotional yearnings of Maya, though they live together yet, as a matter of fact, Gautama knows very little about her. In order to console her he offers a cup of tea without realising Maya's shattered state of mind.

1. Anita Desai, *Cry the Peacock*, Delhi, Orient Paperbacks, 1980, p. 10. Henceforth the novel is referred to in the abbreviated form *CP*.

This mechanical gesture only makes her to brood over Gautama's insensitivity :

> Showing how little he knows of my misery, or how to comfort me. But then, he knew that concerned me. Giving me an opal ring to wear on my finger, he did not notice the translucent skin beneath, the blue flashing veins that ran under and out of the bridge of gold (Emphasis added) ... telling me to go to sleep while he worked at his papers, he did not give another thought to me ... it is his hardness — no, no, not hardness, but the distance he coldly keeps from me. His coldness, his coldness, and incessant talk of cups of tea and philosophy in order not to hear me talk and talking reveal myself. It is that my loneliness in this house (*CP*, p. 9).

This example certainly gives us an idea of Anita Desai's art of reading woman's psychic self, which reveals Maya's inner thoughts. Maya is a hypersensitive woman, an introvert.

Many critics have pointed out this incompatibility. Usha Pathania tracing the cause of disharmony between the characters remark :

> Marital relationships are established with the explicit purpose of providing companionship to each other. However, the element of companionship is sadly missing in the relationship between Maya and Gautama.''[2]

To sum-up, Maya's tragedy is mainly caused by her loneliness, lack of proper response from her husband, non-reciprocation of feeling between the husband and wife, her childlessness and her hypersensitivity. Maya on the one extreme is fragile, with deep cultural roots and refined sensibilities. On the other extreme is her friend Pom who absolutely does not bother and is a typical woman with love for clothes, jewellery, colour, looks, ''Lust for newness, for brightness, colour and gaiety.'' Maya describes her as living in her painted world where there were no shadows of family, tradition and superstition :

> Logic, tact, diplomacy — nothing mattered to her who chattered so glibly and gaily all the day long, jumping up now and then to bring out a new pair of shoes, a new set of rings to show me, talking with eagerness, and animation of anything that was new and bright, and never, never referring to family, tradition, custom,

2. Usha Pathania, ''Human Bonds and Bondages'', *The Fiction of Anita Desai and Kamala Markandeya*, Delhi, Kanishka Publishing House, 1992, p. 14.

> superstitions, all that I dreaded now. I was certain she hated such talks as much as I did, even if she had no reason to fear them. Such things simply did not stop over the bright enamelled horizon of her painted world, for such things bore shadows, and shadows were alien to her ... (*CP*, p. 61).

Yet another variety is that of cabaret dancers who earn their livelihood through their bodies, sometimes only by displaying and sometimes by selling them. The cabaret girls in the novel are what have been described in Sanskrit as *Roopa Jeevas* because they live by their beauty. Although the cabaret girls do not have all the qualities of a *Ganika,* courtesan as described in *Kam Sutra*, yet they have dancing skill with emphasis on showing their fleshy wares. Maya has nothing but disgust for them but they are described well. The female body which has been stock theme of poetry both in English and Sanskrit has been reduced here to a saleable commodity :

> ...''Their portruberent posteriors, and of which they made much, arousing chuckles of delight...bouncing movement that made her bosom more prominent ... so that more and more of that white, tallow flesh would rear out of her blouse ... with a little provocative upthrust of her rump, etc. Their provocative display and movements such as though says, ''See what I have? Like it? Take it, gentleman, take it, it's yours !'' ...''Beautiful ! B-beautiful b-bitch !'' (*CP*, p. 85).

Another character in the novel is Maya's friend Leila who has married a tubercular man against the wishes of her parents. She is a teacher in a girls' school. She married a man knowing his disease. Her attitude towards life is fatalistic. She is gloomy and ascetic wearing no jewellery or bangles. She is a contrast to Pom. In her fatalism there is a masochistic strain. Desai aptly comments that she ''was one of those who require a cross, cannot walk without one'' (*CP*, p. 58).

If Maya is obsessed with the albino priest's prediction, Leila has accepted her destiny and does not grudge or complain ''it was all written in my fate long ago.'' (*CP* p. 59). If Maya is the pampered child, Leila's parent have broken all relations with her. They ''had not seen her, written to her, or in any way communicated with her since the day of her elopement'' (*CP*, p. 58).

Anita Desai not only explores and portrays the feminine psyche of a common woman but also of the subnormal bordering on abnormal woman. These are the women who because of various factors are under so much of mental stress that they cannot be called insane, but then certainly they are not totally normal. The first character that comes to our mind is that of Maya who is hypersensitive and because of her loneliness she is almost a mental wreck. She dreads that she would lose her mental balance and when she is so much lost in herself without moving for a long time. Gautama says :

> "Still sitting there? You haven't stirred out?
>
> Haven't lifted up a book, your sewing? Nothing at all? But this is madness, Maya."
>
> "Madness?" I screamed, leaping up at him, to strike him, to stab him... and began to cry hysterically (*CP*, p. 178).

Although we are informed just after this that Maya is not sure whether the event actually took place but what is certain is her mental chaos. Through the use of unpleasant animal imagery Anita Desai depicts the neurotic state of her mind. The impression given is that of mental fever when she sees weird, things. The image of a lizard, a repulsive creature, has been repeated in the novel. For example : In Chapter VI we find :

> Will it be fire? Will it be flood? Will the lizards rise out of the desert to come up — on us — either upon him or upon myself — with lashing tails and sliding tongues, to crush us beneath their bellies?
>
> Will there be blood? Will there be screams?
>
> And when? When? (*CP*, p. 179).

Here the imagery reveals a sick mind. The image of lizard occurs again after two pages. This time the image is realistic but later it is followed by another weird image of rats which clearly suggests Maya's mental breakdown :

> And yet, in the neck of the lizard spanned above me on the ceiling, its pulse throbbed, and seemed a giant pulse for so small a creature, beating furiously as though it were holding its breath till its blood boiled. And then, in the very height of stillness, its tail switched. One small, brief twitch. But I saw it, and immediately a thousand rats twitched their tails — long, gray, germ-ridden. Just once, before they were still again, stiff (*CP*, p. 183).

There are several other examples of such weird animal imagery used for externalising the mental state of Maya. Later in the novel after she had pushed off Gautama from the roof top she goes back to her father's house in Lucknow. She retreats into the world of her childhood, absolutely cut-off from the present reality. She becomes a girl again lost in her world of picture books and toys:

> ...Child-like serenity of the girl, Maya, who sat somewhere upstairs, delightedly opening cupboards, pulling out drawers, falling upon picture-books and photographs with high, shrill cries of pleasure hugging them to her, dancing around the room with them, on air-borne feet. Now in the silence they could hear her moving above them, like a poltergeist, light and quick on its feet, eager in its chuckles of merriment, and frantic in its ceaseless movements, like a being that is hunted (*CP*, pp. 212-13).

This mental retrogression suggests that Maya has not been able to adjust herself in the world of reality and after killing her husband, she mentally goes back of her protected and pampered childhood, the best part of her life. Thus in the character of Maya, Anita Desai has presented the feminine psyche of both a girl and a woman.

Anita Desai's second novel *Voices in the City* (1965) has received adequate critical response. The title of the novel has made critics to debate on the point whether Nirode or the city of Calcutta may be called the hero of the novel. Desai's skilful handling invests the city with a character. Nirode's sketch on the other hand is rather insipid. Discussed in depth by A.V. Krishna Rao who also feels that it is Calcutta which is the hero of the novel and not Nirode :

> Thus although one may be tempted to consider Nirode as the hero of the novel, the city of Calcutta is indeed the invisible protagonist of the novel. Calcutta, conceived as a force of creation, preservation and destruction is ultimately identified as a symbol for the Goddess Kali."[3]

It is true that the city of Calcutta is the locale for most of the actions of the novel, and serves as a background, and it influences and affects all the major characters in the novel. But the novel itself is primarily a family drama around which the story revolves. Even the blurb of the novel says that the novel describes the corrosive effects of the city life upon the Indian family. The whole novel is divided into four sections — 'Nirode', 'Monisha', 'Amla' and 'Mother'. This chapter division tells us that in spite of the important role played by

3. A.V. Krishna Rao, "*Voices in the City* : A Study," *Perspectives on Anita Desai*, Ed. Ramesh K. Srivastava, Ghaziabad, Vimal Prakashan, 1981, p. 175.

the city of Calcutta, the novel is more concerned with the characters than with the background. Although this section division refers to four characters only, yet primarily it is the story of Nirode.

Voices in the City is "The unforgettable story of a Bohemian brother and his two sisters caught in the cross currents of changing social values". It is a feudal family of Kalimpong dominated by the mother with an inferior father who is most of the time drunk; there are four children, two sons and two daughters — Arun, Nirode, Monisha and Amla. The story of the novel begins with the departure of Arun to England for higher studies and Nirode who works in a newspaper office as a simple clerk. His sister Monisha is married to Jiban a middle-rung officer in a Government department with a large joint family, this is a typical middle class family. The younger sister Amla has received training as a commercial artist in Bombay and has come to Calcutta to join an advertisement firm. Father is no more now, mother leads a lonely life because all the children are outside Kalimpong; she gets company of her neighbour, one retired Major Chaddha with whom seemingly she is also having an affair which is much resented by Nirode. Nirode's life as presented in the novel is a succession of failures, from bringing out a magazine called *Voice* to writing of a play, opening a book stall, and even selling spurious antique art pieces. Amla has a short-lived affair with a married artist Dharma and through her we are shown the world of the upper class society. Monisha's ill-matched marriage, her loneliness, sterility, and the stress of living in a joint family with an insensitive husband push her to the breaking point and she commits suicide by self-immolation. The novel ends with the funeral of Monisha on arrival of her mother from Kalimpong.

In this novel also Anita Desai has portrayed feminine psyche mainly through the character of Monisha, although there are other women characters also in the novel. Monisha is similar to Maya in that she is also childless, sensitive and a victim of ill-matched marriage. If Maya is lonely in her family because it is a nuclear family with no one except her husband Monisha's family has too many people, since it is a joint family. The over-crowded house makes her uneasy and even though she has a room of her own, literally yet metaphorically she hasn't, for the women of the family just never bother that the daughter-in-law may some time need privacy. Her sisters-in-law always without any hesitation barge into her room making themselves comfortable on the big bed discussing Monisha's sarees and her blocked fallopian tubes. Her plight increases because sterility is a stigma for a married woman. Through Monisha, Anita Desai has portrayed the psyche of a sensitive intellectual woman who is suffocated in uncongenial atmosphere of her in-laws' house. She is happy neither with her husband nor with his family members. She seems to have been transplanted in the wrong soil. Because of her intellectual nature she is not much interested in religion even though she reads the *Bhagwad Geeta*. Several *Shlokas* from it have been quoted. Had she been a believer, her anguish and plight would have been reduced but it is not so as she writes in her diary :

> If I had religious faith, I could easily enough renounce all this. But I have no faith, no alternative to my confused despair, there is nothing I can give myself to, and so I must stay. The family here, and their surroundings, tell me such a life cannot be lived – a life dedicated to nothing – that his husk is a protection from death.
>
> Ah yes, yes, then it is a choice between death and mean existence, and that, surely, is not a difficult choice.''[4]

She is in contrast with the average Bengali daughter-in-law as described graphically in the same section, sacrificing her life for the husband and the family confined within the four walls of the house. The life of a woman like Monisha in the given circumstances is never happy and the result is that she burns herself to death. Her impending death by suicide has been poetically described by Anita Desai even before her actual death which comes later in the novel. She yearns for eternal darkness beyond sleep because even sleep may have nightmares. She feels herself totally submerged in darkness, she does't want even the stars to which she has referred in the context of what separates her from Jiban's family.

> Leave me to gather the stars, frosty and distant and cool. Leave me to gather and then to reject them. Queenly. I'll have only the darkness. Only the dark spaces between the stars, for they are the only thing on the earth that can comfort me, rub a balm into my wounds, into my throbbing head, and bring me this coolness, this stillness, this interval of peace. Even sleep has not this sweet, swaying stillness as these immensities of the night, sky to which I tip my face, allowing them to fall into my eyes, and fall. Sleep has nightmares. This, this empty darkness, has not so

4. Anita Desai, *Voices in the City*, Delhi, Orient Paperbacks, 1965, Henceforth the novel is referred to in the abbreviated from as *VC*.

much as a dream. It is one untitled waste, a desert to which my heart truly belongs.[5]

The above abstract has Shakespearean echo from *Hamlet* when Hamlet is pondering over suicide in the famous "to be or not to be" soliloquy.

In exact contrast to Monisha is another minor character Sarla who is the wife of Nirode's affluent friend who lives in a large victorian house with the shadows and remembrance of the days of the East India Company. She is also fond of drinks and is described as "a voluptuous porpoise of ebony flesh" having, in words of her husband, "too many admirer...white ones — mainly, and a few that she calls honey-complexion" (ed) (34). But Nirode dislikes her and to him "she seemed to belong to the same century as her house, to that class of courtesans who had clung like bracelets, or vampires, to its wealth and leisure and decadence" (*VC*, p. 34). She may not be like the cabaret girls of the *Cry the Peacock* but she belongs to that class which believes in the philosophy of 'eat, drink, and be merry.'

Monisha's mother also did not have a happy marital life because of her ill-matched marriage. In the eyes of Amla her mother is "the most beautiful woman in the world, and very accomplished. None of us is like her, so polished and balanced and contained like a well-cut jewel" (*VC*, p. 209). She has refined taste for flowers, music and good food. The father is a kind of sadist deriving pleasure in hurting her. After the husband's death when there is no restriction on her, she becomes free and carries on an affair with a retired Major, Chadha much to Nirode's anger and hatred. Even though Nirode apparently hates his mother yet he too is fascinated by her beauty even in her declining years.

Motherhood is the ultimate objective of the woman and that is why the importance of and craving for children, if male, all the better is feelingly described by the novelist. Anita Desai has explored the psyche of both the childless women, as of Maya in *Cry the Peacock*, of Monisha in *Voices in the City*, and also of women with children, like Sita in *Where Shall We Go this Summer* and Nanda Kaul in *Fire on the Mountain*. The interesting thing to note is that Anita Desai has portrayed also the psyche of, "unwomanly" women in the sense that they don't want children. Certainly they are not as "unsexed" as lady Macbeth was.

5. *Ibid.*, p. 138.

Sita in *Where Shall We Go this Summer* shudders at the idea of giving birth to a fifth child. She becomes so upset that she withdraws into her psyche of childhood days on the magic island. Against all sane advice she goes to the island in advanced stage of pregnancy. She lives in the world of fantasy thinking that going to the island and thereby to the world of childhood she could prevent the biological process of delivery. If Maya is starved of children, for her :

> "Children... Through her mind flowed a white, flapping succession in nappies, vests... that would have to be gathered together. She could see the expressionless faces of the night nurses in the gynae ward... in the greenish night light, regarding her as she came in, ravaged by the first pains... She could see the impassive face of nurses who would stay by her in the theatre, now and then glancing at her large, flat watch, bored by yet another woman's panic-stricken labour (*WSWGS*, pp. 153-154).

Here is a strange case of neuroticism where the woman doesn't want to give birth to a child. However, finally she consents to the sane advice of her husband and comes back to Bombay to deliver. Sita in *Where Shall We Go this Summer* also suffers from ill-matched marriage but the fault lies more with her rather than with the husband who is considerate and tries to make her happy. It is another matter that because of her pathological sensitivity she is always high-strung. Raman is a businessman living in a joint family. Raman's family members are quite accommodative and considerate towards Sita but she is always grudging. Raman's is a traditional Hindu family where even men do not smoke openly but Sita just to spite her in-laws smokes openly. Things become so bad that Raman shifts to a flat to avoid daily tensions. But even here Sita is not happy. She is irrational childish, and petulant. She becomes upset even after reading the newspaper which is full of the news of brutality and violence and destruction all over the world :

> "...her husband casually handed her the newspaper on his way out to office. They all hammered at her with cruel fists — the fallen blocks, the torn watercolours, the headlines about the war in Vietnam, the photograph of a woman weeping over a small grave, another of a crowd outside a Rhodesian jail; articles about the perfidy of Pakistan... They were handgrenades all, hurled at her frail gold fish bowl belly and instinctively she laid her hands over it, feeling the child there play like some soft-fleshed fish in a bowl of warm sea-water... frightened certain

> now that civilisation had been created by the god-like efforts of the few, in the face of a constant, timeless war of destruction that had begun with time and was now roaring around her, battering her and her fish-foetus so that survival seemed hopeless. How could civilisation survive, how could the child? How could she hold them whole and pure and unimpeached in the midst of this bloodshed? They would surely be wounded, fall and die."[6]

Being sensitive to violence and brutality in the world is one thing but to be affected by it so much as not to lead a normal life is a different thing bordering on mental disease. In the novel we find other instances also where apparently trivial things upset Sita's composure. For instance, once a wounded eagle sits on the ledge of window and is attacked by crows. Seeing this Sita becomes agitated and tries to scare-away the crows by using a toy gun. Her daughter Menka sometimes sketches and paints them. Once she does not like one of her paintings and tears it away. Even this upsets Sita, even the usual fights and quarrels between the children annoy her and when "her sons hurled their bodies at each other as if they were made for attack and combat" she screams but they do not stop. Menka the sensitive girl said, "They are only playing." Sita said, "That is no way of playing... Get-up, Get-*up* stop it" (*WSWGS*, pp. 44-45).

Through the character of Sita in *Where Shall We Go this Summer* and Maya in *Cry the Peacock*, Anita Desai has portayed the feminine psyche of neurotic women. The cause of their mental disbalance is different. However, both of them are not normal. They might be called sub-normal, if not abnormal. In Maya's case the psychological probing is more detailed whereas in Sita's case it is not so. What is remarkable about Anita Desai's psychological probings of the women is that she includes females of different age groups. It is not that she confines herself to the young or the middle-aged. She has also perceptively explored the psyche of a girl in *Fire on the Mountain*.

Raka is the girl who occupies our attention in *Fire on the Mountain*. It is difficult to say whether the novel centres around Nanda Kaul or Raka. Certainly the novel begins with the focus on Nanda Kaul but in the course of the novel the focus shifts on to Raka. The title also refers to her, for it is she who sets the forest on fire, hence, fire on the Mountain. Raka is an unusual child, her name

6. Anita Desai, *Fire on the Mountain*, London, Penguin Books, 1977, pp. 55-56. Henceforth the novel is referred to in the abbreviated form *FOM*.

does not correspond with any of her physical characteristics :

> *Raka* — What an utter misnomer thought Nanda Kaul... Raka meant the moon, but this child was not roundfaced, calm of radiant... Nanda Kaul thought she looked like one of those dark crickets that leap up in fright but do not sing, or a mosquito, minute and fine, on thin, precarious legs.''[7]

If Nanda Kaul defends her privacy fiercely Raka too is absolutely independent, satisfied with her own self and never bothering her Nani. She is so self-absorbed that any effort on Nanda Kaul's part to attract her completely fails, even her fantastic tales. She is the most unchildlike child. Nothing appeals to her. She was ''the child who never played games.'' Instead of listening to the fanciful tales from Nanda Kaul she prefers to go out doors all by herself, roaming in the desolate hills and forest. She is obliquely defiant, and she is mistress of herself. Once coming from her usual ramblings through the hills and forests she speaks to herself, ''I don't care — I don't care — I don't care for *anything.*'' Her unchildlike quality and introvert nature is the result of her traumatic childhood. Once she stealthily goes down the hill to the club of the Research station on a moon-lit night and while she spies on the drunken Orgy in the club her mind is flooded with the unpleasant memory of her childhood days, of her drunken father coming home late at night and beating her mother and she hiding somewhere in the room.

> ... her father, home from a party, stumbling and crashing through the curtains of night, his mouth opening to let out a flood of rotten stench, beating at her mother with hammers and fists of abuse-harsh filthy abuse that made Raka cover under her bed clothes and wet the mattress in fright, feeling the stream of urine warm and weakening between her legs like a stream of blood, and her mother lay down on the floor and shut her eyes and wept. Under her feet, in the dark, Raka felt that flat, wet jelly of her mother's being squelching and quivering, so that she didn't know where to put her feet and wept as she tried to get free of it. Ahead of her, no longer on the ground but at some distance now, her mother was crying. Then it was a jackal crying (*FOM*, pp. 71-72).

It is this traumatic childhood experience that has such a dehumanising effect on Raka's mind that she becomes a pathetic to finding any

7. Anita Desai, *Fire on the Mountain*, London, Penguin Books, 1977, p. 39. Henceforth the novel is referred to in the abbreviated form *FOM*.

interest in childish games and there is nothing childlike in her character. It is significant that several animal images have been used in relation to her. Her refusal to play with toys which is so natural with the children very well describes her psyche. On the other extreme of the exploration and portrayal of feminine psyche is the character of the senile Meera Masi in *Clear Light of Day* which is an equally gripping characterisation. The ageing Meera Masi picks-up the habit of drinking alcohol and when she does not get it she steals it and when in her drunken stupor she tears off her clothes becoming naked showing her shrunken breasts, wasted body with white pubic hair she is really a pathetic figure, a mockery of dignity of conventional graceful old age. Had Robert Browning seen her he would not have written, "Grow old along with me", the best is yet to come, etc.

Nanda Kaul's case in *Fire on the Mountain* is in between the two. She has raised a big family with full responsibility but in the evening of her life she loves seculsion and the news of her grand-daughter Raka's arrival shatters her isolated world. Raka who is a precarious child from a broken home presents another facet of feminine psyche. She is a fine study of a disturbed child, withdrawn, not interested in childish games. She is more interested in rambling through hills and jungles. Her disturbed mental state culminates in her act of pyromania when at the end of the novel she puts the forest on fire. Hence the title of the novel.

Anita Desai has also touched upon a very vital aspect of the feminine-psyche, *viz.* the erotic. Maya is not only childless but also sexually unsatisfied. Anita Desai's handling of erotic is very subtle, absolutely unlike Kamala Markandeya, Kamala Das and Shobha Dey. In *Cry the Peacock* this is how the novelist describes Maya's desire for carnal pleasure

> "...longing to be with him, be close to him... make haste in undressing... But when I went to rouse him from the couch, with a touch, I saw that he had closed his eyes not with mere tiredness, but in profound, invulnerable sleep, and was very far from any world of mine, however enticing (*CP*, p. 93).

If Maya is denied sexual pleasure there is on the other end Sita who hates sex. For her it is animal-like not worth her notice. It is a different thing that she has given birth to four children and the fifth is on way. For Sita down to earth man like her husband and his friends are so gross that "they are *nothing* — nothing but appetite and sex. Only food, sex and money matter, animals" (*WSWGS*, p. 17). They are even nearest to animals when Raman asks, "I thought you liked animals." She bursts out :

> "My pet animals – or wild animals in the forest, yes. But these are neither – they are like pariahs you see in the streets, hanging about drains and dustbins, waiting to pounce and kill and eat" (*WSWGS*, p. 17).

Mira Masi in *Clear Light of Day* is a widow, a distant relative of the Dasa's and even though she is a minor character, in her we find another example of sexually unsatisfied woman. She became a widow when young and had she been pretty she must have become a victim of sexual exploitation by her husband's brother. This is another facet of feminine psyche.

Her latest novel *Baumgartner's Bombay* is about Baumgartner the hero, but through the character of Lotte, his friend, we find another aspect of feminine psyche, that of a kept. She is the kept of a Calcutta-based Marvari Seth, Kantilal who maintains her in Bombay and comes periodically to her for booze and sex. Lotte in her declining years initiates sex with Baumgartner and he obliges. In her case it is physical need.

In different novels Anita Desai has portrayed different facets of human feminine psyche. Her range of characters in this regard is quite wide as we have seen above. Her characters cover women of almost all age groups. In Raka we have a child going to girlhood. In Maya a married woman, in Lotte a middle aged woman and in Nanda Kaul, and Ila Das old woman. Not only are the women of different age groups but they are also of different types and characters. If Monisha is an intellectual type, Maya is hypersensitive, we have Sarla in *In Custody* who cannot look beyond the four walls of her house. Even though the wife of a Hindi lecturer she has absolutely no interest in literature, or her husband's profession. She is so ignorant that she concludes her husband's frequent visits to Delhi to interview the poet as a ruse for meeting his girl- friend. In *Voices in the City*, we also find subtle suggestions of adultery between the widow mother of Monisha and the retired Major Chadha. Thus we can say that Anita Desai has done well in exploring different aspects of feminine psyche.

Chapter III

FAMILIAL RELATIONSHIPS

In the preceding chapter we have seen how Anita Desai has explored different aspects of feminine psyche which also includes familial relationships. In this chapter we would study the woman in relation to her family, assuming different roles. It is but natural for a writer like Anita Desai to make family the centre of her novels and this applies to her almost every novel although the degree may vary. In a novel like *Baumgartner's Bombay*, which is the story of a rootless man without family in India. The family is very much present, although not in realistic term but at the mental level in the mind of the hero Baumgartner.

It is the story of a man who is persecuted by society both in his own country and in his adopted country, of course, for entirely different reasons. In his native Germany he is a victim of racial prejudice simply because he is a Jew. In India he is never accepted by the society even though he has lived in this country for several decades. When his father's flourishing furniture-business is destroyed by fanatical Nazis, he is advised to try his luck in colonial India. He comes to Calcutta and for some time he does well in the timber business. But then the Second World War breaks out and even though he has nothing to do with Nazi Germany, because he holds a German passport, he is arrested as an alien citizen of a hostile country. He is put in captivity along with other Germans for six years in a camp in the foothills of the Himalayas. When he is released after the war, he goes to Calcutta only to find the city scorched by communal frenzy attendant on the partition of the country. He comes to Bombay and settles down there, living an ascetic life. In the late sixties and early seventies when India was littered with so many hippies or 'flower children' he is ironically and pathetically killed by a German drug addict hippy whom out of human consideration he had taken to his house. The tragedy is all the more acute, for Baumgartner is killed for a small amount of money that the hippy would get for his drug, by selling a few silver, or silver coated trophies which he steals from Baumgartner's house. Desai ends the novel here.

In India Baumgartner is rootless not only because he is in a foreign country but also because he is familyless. He is unmarried and directs his affection towards the cats that he keeps in his house. Each cat has been given a name. Ironically it is not the human but the cats which are Baumgartner's family. However, he carries happy memories of his family when he was a child in Berlin. He was brought up in a congenial family with a prosperous father and a cultured mother. His family is much unlike the usual families described in Anita Desai's novels. His mother was affectionate and he recollects how she would take him to her relative in the suburbs of Berlin and the memory of such visits even after long years is still there in Baumgartner's mind. It would be no exaggeration to say that in an alien country the memory of his happy childhood sustains him emotionally. He has preserved letters from his mother which came to him regularly before the outbreak of the Second World War. In the very first chapter of the novel these letters are described. The letters were almost like sacred relics for Baumgartner. The second chapter of the novel describes his happy childhood and here we come across his going out with his father. There is an interesting description when his father offers him a sip of beer and certainly a child cannot appreciate the taste of beer and this makes his father laugh :

> "Smiling at the disbelieving look in his eyes, the hesitation that held his upper lip rigid, his father slid the mug of beer towards him. 'No one's looking,' he said with a wink, 'quick now,' and Hugo climbed on to his knees — they were fat and the edge of the bench made two welts across them — and bent over the pewter mug to draw the froth in through his lips. It was cold, bitter, smelt of wet straw and tasted of steel. It's gleaming metal knife cut across his tongue and made him gasp and withdraw, froth-moustached, to make his father laugh as he never laughed at home."[1]

---

1. Anita Desai, *Baumgartner's Bombay*, Harmondsworth, Penguin Books, 1989, p. 24. Henceforth the novel is referred to in the abbreviated form *BB*.

The above extract shows the happy childhood of Baumgartner, something uncommon in the novels of Anita Desai. He is also reminded of several expressions of endearment for him by his mother. These expressions are in German which is but natural because it is his mother tongue. And as most of such expressions are absurd so also is his case when he is called a little mouse by his mother : " *'Meine Kleine Maus,' 'Mein Haschen,' 'Liebchen ...*" (*BB*, p. 3). In the novel several German poems are used which are children's poems which describe the happy childhood of Baumgartner. The mood is expressed by:

> *'Hopp, hopp, hopp*
>
> *Pferdchen lauf galopp'* (*BB*, p. 25).

Baumgartner also keeps in his mind other loving expressions from his mother for him for example the one describing his dark eyes. But in this instance the description is not very happy because it has been used in the context of his being an outcast in India because of his physical features. In Germany his dark eyes were unusual for a German but in India where generally people have dark eyes and dark hair he is considered an outsider because of his fairskin. The following description shows his plight. What was a disqualification in Germany remains the same in India for a different reason. He could have dyed his hair but not his eyes:

> .... What could he have done about his eyes? It was not that they were blue far from it, his mother, holding him on her knee and clapping hands in a game, had called them dark eyes, *dunkele Augen,* 'but Indians did not seem to think them so (*BB,* p. 20).

This is just an example of how a family physical characteristic, or to be more precise physical feature may become a source of disadvantages. The above situation shows that even though Baumgartner enjoys good familial relationship, yet because of circumstances he is cut off from his family. His father disappeared right before him when he was a child, thanks to the Nazi regime, and both for his survival and economic prospects he had to leave his country of origin for good and thus was separated from his mother, the only familial relationship that he was left with. In *Baumgartner's Bombay* we came across a pathetic novel that deals with a broken family not because of the fault of family members but because of socio-political reasons over which the individual has no control. He does try to have a surrogate family in Bombay with the family of Chaman Lal. But so long as Chaman Lal is alive his family tolerates him. The moment he dies he is thrown out. Baumgartner's case is similar to that of Lotte who had taken great pains and was devoted to the family of Kanti Lal whose kept she was. But just after his death she ceases to have any claim over his family. She was devoted to Kanti Lal and his family and she would take care of his sons like a mother but after Kanti's death his family members refuse to recognise her :

> "Those boys I know them when they were little. If they were sick, I made them porridge. At night I sat holding ice to their foreheads.... Not even a thermometer they had in the house till I went and got one. If they wanted to dress smart, I went and chose their clothes" (*BB*, p. 77).

After Kanti's death nothing is the same. His sons refuse to recognise her, "who is this woman? We don't know this woman. Throw her out" (77). Lotte's tragedy is that she is not a part of the family legally and being a foreigner, she is not even able to express her sympathy to the dying man who had maintained her lavishly and would periodically come from Calcutta to visit her. Worse still when she goes to Calcutta during the last days of Kanti she is not even allowed to go to the hospital :

> "In Calcutta, I was not even there to hold his hand. His family was already fighting over the property – no one even to hold his hand, there in the hospital. Dogs die like that, in the street" (*BB*, p. 73).

Lotte's case and her relationship with the Kanti Lal family is ironical. Here is a case of unfulfilled familial relationship. These two examples acquaint us with Anita Desai's fine portrayal of familial relationships.

In ancient India we had polygamy and the *Shastras* described the duties of a co-wife but in modern times bigamy is a crime. But man being polygamous in nature he at times carries on life-long relationship with the other woman. In this connection we are reminded of another novel *Fire on the Mountain* in which Prof. Kaul the vice-chancellor and husband of Nanda Kaul carries on a love affair with Miss David, the arithmetic teacher. But as she was a Christian he could not dare break social code and marry her. The novel was awarded the Sahitya Akademi Award for 1978 and thus it brought recognition to Anita Desai. The novel which also won the Royal Society Award has a very thin plot.

Nanda Kaul, the widow of a vice-chancellor, is compelled both by choice and circumstances to live in a secluded old bungalow 'Carignano', in Kasauli, fiercely guarding her seclusion and privacy. But her insulated life is stirred by the arrival of her great grand-daughter Raka, a girl of seven or eight years, an introvert, sensitive as Nanda herself. She is very much confined to her own self, resenting any intimacy with Nanda. She busies herself with rambling through deserted hills and gorges, she is specially attracted towards a burnt house and is preoccupied with the idea of a forest-fire. A childhood friend of Nanda, Ila Das who has fallen on bad days, is a social worker in a nearby village. She comes to tea with Nanda one afternoon. They have long chat about their early days, their experiences as a social worker, and as the vice-chancellor's wife respectively. She now lives in penury. On her way back it gets dark and near her village Preet Singh, who was dissuaded by her not to marry his minor daughter with an old man, is waiting in ambush. Angered by Ila Das's opposition to the marriage, he strangulates her and later rapes her. Nanda is informed telephonically about the outrage by the police inspector. She is still to digest this shocking news when Raka comes to say that she has set the forest on fire. And this is the end of the novel. Anita Desai excels in the poetic portrayal of the locale with charred trees, desolate landscape, dusty road, rain and the like. The novel is full of animal and nature imagery.

Like Lotte, Nanda too could not legally belong to the family and she is no better than a kept. In this case the blame goes to the cowardice of Prof. Kaul who just gave lip service to marital life. Outwardly the Kaul's were an ideal couple to university community but from inside it was all empty, the whole social role and socialising was a mere sham :

> "Not had her husband loved and cherished her and kept her like a queen – he had only done enough to keep her quiet while he carried on a lifelong affair with Miss David, the mathematics mistress whom he had not married because she was a Christian but whom he had loved, all his life loved."[2]

Because of her husband's cowardice and selfishness Nanda Kaul had to suffer. She readily discharges her duty towards the family but in doing so loses her individuality and identity. Like Sita of *Where Shall We Go This Summer*? Although to a lesser degree, Nanda Kaul is not very happy in coping with the large family and unending stream of guests.

2. Anita Desai, *Fire on the Mountain*, London, Penguin Books, p. 145. Henceforth the novel is referred to in the abbreviated form *FOM*.

"And her children – the children were all alien to her nature. She neither understood nor loved them. She did not live here alone by choice — she lived here alone because that was what she was forced to do, reduced to doing " (*FOM*, p. 145).

She is so busy raising the family and discharging the duties of mother, housewife and hostess that in the evening of her life she is happy in her seclusion even though it is partly volantary and partly circumstantial. When the news of her grand-daughter Raka's arrival comes she hates being disturbed by the arrival of the uninvited guest. It doesn't matter that the person coming is her own flesh and blood. In the fifth chapter of the novel when she is looking back at her life we find that through and through she is only pretending, wearing a personae, acting a role which is imposed on her. In the following extract the difference between appearance and reality is made very clear. Our apology for this lengthy quotation lies in the fact that aspect of difference between the surface and inner reality is crucial to Desai's thematic thrust :

"Looking down, over all those years she had survived and borne, she saw them, not bare and shining as the plains below, but like the gorge, cluttered, choked and blackened with the heads of children and grand-children, servants and guests, all restlessly surging, clamouring about her.

She thought of the veranda of their house in the small university town in Punjab, the vice-chancellor's house over which she had presided with such an air as to strike awe into visitors who came to call and leave them slightly gaping. She had her cane chair there, too, and she had sat there, not still and emptily, but mending clothes, sewing on strings and buttons and letting out hems, at her feet a small charcoal brazier on which a pot of *kheer* bubbled, snipping threads and instructing the servant girl to stir, stir, don't stop stirring or it'll burn, and then someone had to be called to hold the smallest child from falling into the bubbling pot and carry it away, screaming worse than if it were scalded. Into this din, a tonga had driven up and disgorged a flurry of guests in their visiting saris, all to flap their palm-leaf handfans as they sat in a ring about her – the wives and daughters of the lecturers and professors over whom her husband ruled. She thought of that hubbub and of how she had managed and how everyone had said, pretending to think she couldn't hear but really wanting her to, 'Isn't she splendid? Isn't

> she like a queen? Really, vice-chancellor is lucky to have a wife who can run everything as she does, and her eyes had flashed when she heard, like a pair of black blades, wanting to cut them, despising them, crawling grey bugs about her fastidious feet. That was the look no one had dared catch or return.
>
> Looking down at her knuckles, two rows of yellow bones on the railing, she thought of her sons and daughters, of her confinements, some in great discomfort at home and others at the small filthy missionary-run hospital in the bazaar, and the different nurses and doctors who had wanted to help her but never could, and the slovenly, neurotic ayahs she had to have because there was such a deal of washing and ironing to do and Mr. Kaul had wanted her always in silk, at the head of the long rosewood table in the dining-room, entertaining his guests.
>
> Mentally she stalked through the rooms of that house — his house, never hers — very carefully closing the wire-screen doors behind her to keep out the flies, looking sharply to see if the dark furniture, all rosewood, had been polished and the doors of the gigantic cupboards properly shut. She sniffed to make sure the cook was not smoking *biris* in the kitchen and to verify that all the metalware smelt freshly of Brasso.
>
> She seemed to hear poignant shrieks from the canna beds in the garden – a child had tumbed off the swing, another had been stung by a swasp, a third slapped by the fourth — and gone out on the veranda to see them come wailing up the steps with cut lips, bruised knees, broken teeth and tears, and bent over them with that still, ironic bow to duty that no one had noticed or defined.

Thus in Nanda Kaul's case familial relationship is not genuine although it may appear to be so.

In her very first novel *Cry the Peacock* we find the heroine Maya in several roles discharging different familial duties. She is a pampered child who has been brought up in a fairy world, ill-equipped to cope with reality. Things become all the worse when she is married to a down-to-earth rational husband. She is a motherless child and that is why she does not grow into a balanced personality. Since she is childless herself her predicament becomes all the more acute. We see her in the role of a wife, daughter, sister and sister-in-law. In this novel also we find something amiss in familial relationship, specially with her in-laws. With a busy husband, uninterested in her feelings and emotions. She is totally out of tune with her surroundings. Being childless she is in dire need of the cosy-refuge of familial relationship but unfortunately everyone is too preoccupied to spare time for her. Her mother-in-law, who visits her and whom she wants to stay back to alleviate her lonely existence refuses to do so. She has her own varied excuses. She is a social worker involved in several activities of social service and therefore she says :

> "How can I, child?... . It is impossible."[3]

Being motherless she wants a mother figure which is readily available in her mother-in-law. She desires for the company of her mother-in-law and sister-in-law :

> "... If they stayed a while, they might help me, as my own father could not, by teaching me some of that marvellous indifference to everything that was not vital, immediate and present, I did not know how they could do this but somehow it had to be done" (*CP*, p. 162).

In spite of her refusal to stay back Maya is unable to forget her mother-in-law in whom she finds mother substitute. But this relationship becomes pathetic as it is also one-sided. Maya craves for maternal tenderness :

> "And yet I yearned for her to hold me to her bosom. I could not remember my own mother at all. My throat began to swell with unbearable self-pity. I would cry, I knew it, in a while, and dreaded it, in their sane presence. 'Please,' I whispered" (*CP*, p. 163).

If Maya's marital life is unhappy her sister-in-law's marriage is also on the rocks. She wants to seek divorce from her husband and that is why she has come to her brother Gautama who is a lawyer. But subscribing to the old values he doesn't approve of the idea of divorce and feels filing a divorce petition too low for him :

> "... What does she take me for — one of those two-rupee lawyers that squat under the banyan tree outside the courts... I haven't time to waste on a case like hers — the mess she makes by being too bossy and self-willed and bullying."

Thus we find that in *Cry the Peacock* except for father-daughter relationship other familial relationships are not happy. Maya has

---

3. Anita Desai, *Cry the Peacock*, New Delhi, Orient Paperbacks, 1980, p. 163.

happy memories of her brother when they were children but later in the novel he goes away to America to stand on his own legs, leaving the background of a Rai Saheb father.

Like most of her novels in *Where Shall We Go This Summer* the story moves around a family.

The story is of Raman, his wife Sita and four children. The fifth child yet to be born, yet plays an important role in the story. As a matter of fact, the whole story is occasioned by the fifth pregnancy of Sita. Like many of her heroines, Sita's childhood plays an important role in shaping her personality. Her childhood was unusual in the sense that her mother had deserted the family and the father, a freedom-fighter and social worker, was too busy to take care of his children. She lived a life of austerity with limited material comforts, and yet she enjoyed the Arcadian life on the island of Manori in her father's house before her marriage. After the death of her father she was married to Raman, the son of her father's friend Deedar. Deedar arranged this marriage more out of pity than for love to the expectations of Sita. Initially Sita lives in Raman's joint family which is willing to "accept even such an outrageous outsider" like Sita. But because of Sita's haughty, supercilious, unadjusting nature, Raman decides to live separately with his family in a flat. He tries to make Sita happy but she is hard to please and she is always seething with anger, discontent and apathy. When Sita becomes pregnant for the fifth time, it is an ordeal for her, and she does not want to deliver the child. Manori island seems to her the enchanted island of miracles and she decides to go there, against the sane advice of Raman, along with her two children Menaka and Karan even during her advanced stage of pregnancy. On the island she expects a miracle that never comes about because miracles hardly ever take place in real life. They only exist in the fantasy world of children. Actually, her going to the island is symbolically her retrogression to childhood. On the island she broods over her past, fantasising over her childhood and her father who was a god to illiterate islanders. The children get annoyed and are fed up with the primitive life on the island and Menaka asks her father to take them back to Bombay. Raman comes and takes the family away though Sita goes only grudgingly. However, by the end of the novel revelation comes to Sita and she accepts the world of reality and becomes mentally prepared for the delivery of her child. Thus the novel ends establishing victory of reason over fantasy.

Bye-Bye Black Bird is a novel set in England and though from the point of chapter division of the study the novel belongs more to the next chapter, yet the familial relationship is very much there. The novel is about Asian immigrants specially Indians settled in London and thus it has a theme of international ramifications. The internal evidences of the novel do not make it very clear as to how Sarah, the English wife of Adit Sen would fare in India as the daughter-in-law of a leading Bengali family. But one thing is clear that even at the expense of social ostracisation taunts of her colleagues and young pupils she married a brown man. And in doing so she has broken the social code of the British society by marrying a person from India.

In the context of familial relationship we find that Sarah's parents accept her and her husband. But the significant thing about Sarah is that she is a devoted wife and even though she undergoes suffering and mental torture, she doesn't hesitate to leave her native country and go for a good tour to India. This going away is not easy : "She felt all the pangs of saying Good-Bye to her past twenty four years."[4]

It may be realled that in *Where Shall We Go This Summer*? We have two kinds of familial relationships regarding the heroine Sita. Sita's father may not have been a Rai Saheb pampering the child, yet her father carried for her magical aura around her. He was a freedom-fighter whose wife had deserted him, living somewhere in Benares and Sita was brought up in an atmosphere which cannot be, strictly called a family. We have vague suggestions of incest between Sita's father and Rekha her step-sister. The suggestion of incest is not very clear still one can read between the lines :

> "But her father... too quite clearly for it was always the big girl's heavy shoulders that he fondled, her face that he scanned as she sat singing across the room from him... "Sisters should be a *little alike*"... "But you are not sisters,".... "She is only your step-sister".... "But his words had dropped on her skin like acid and she felt them burn whenever she caught an exchange of that heavy-lidded look between father and daughter, or his arm in its fine white sleeve lie fondlingly across her round shoulders".... Perhaps because she never found him alone — always with Rekha silent at his side, or in the centre of a ring of young, fanatic, brilliant-eyed *chelas* who also wore homespun, walked barefoot, and respected,

4. Anita Desai, *Bye-Bye Black Bird*, New Delhi, Orient Paperbacks, 1982, p. 221.

> admired, and adored him. She told herself she could never approach him to ask of such private and, somehow, secret matters. As an adult, later, she asked herself, had there been no opportunity ever of talking alone to him? Ah. She remembered, with an instinctive shrinking from the shock and the pain, a few strange moments, still unexplained.[5]

The novel also has the theme of joint family system, so typical of India. Because of stubborn nature of Sita, she refuses to adjust herself to her husband's family. Her husband who is a practical man in order to avoid daily bickering and tension moves into a flat. Sita's in-laws are accommodating and considerate but she takes perverse delight in teasing them. In her in-laws' family nobody smokes openly but out of spite she starts smoking before the family. Her smoking is symbolic of her unconscious desire to harm the foetus she is carrying. Sita is childish and petulant. She is worse than Maya. At least Maya has reascns to be dissatisfied but here is a woman who lives in her own world of fantasy putting all her family members to trouble. By the end of the novel she consents to rational advice and comes back to Bombay to deliver the baby. In Sita's case too it is a case of bad familial relationship.

B. Ramchandra Rao studies the novel as a dramatisation of "the conflict between two irreconcilable temperaments, of two diametrically opposed attitudes towards life." He concludes by saying :

> The tragedy in *Where Shall We Go This Summer*? arises out of the inability of the characters to connect the prose and the passion in their lives. They have lived only in fragments. The novel ends with a defeated and despondent Sita unable to rediscover the passion of life and deciding to accept the prose of life. But the book ends with the implicit comment that this need not have been the only ending. It could have turned out otherwise.[6]

Thus Rao finds *Where Shall We Go This Summer?* an open ended novel. This is the novelist's device of not being dogmatic of committed towards a conclusion, rather giving the reader a scope for his own reading and conclusion. M.K. Naik comments on Sita and the structure of the novel :

> "*Where Shall We Go This Summer* (1975) marks a return to the autonomous world of inner reality. Sita, the main character here,

5. Anita Desai, *Where Shall We Go this Summer*?, Delhi, Orient Paperbacks, 1982, p. 78-80. Henceforth the novel is referred to in the abbreviated form *WSWGS*.

6. B. Ramchandra Rao, *The Novels of Mrs. Anita Desai : A Study*, New Delhi, Kalyani Publishers, 1977.

appears to be less morbid than Maya after four children. The cruelty and callousness of urban life stiffle her and when she is with child again, she panics at the thought of bringing a new, fragile being into this harsh world and runs away to a small island, which has childhood association for her; but finally allows her husband to persuade her to return. The novel is tightly structured and the island is an evocative symbol of a lost paradise, but Sita's sudden capitulation at the end comes as an anti-climax.''[7]

Another novel that is very much concerned with familial relationship is *Voices in the City*. The novel is more about familial relationship gone sour rather than about fulfilling relationship. Although the title may make one feel that the novel is about the city of Calcutta, and certainly the city has great influence on different characters. But the ''Voices'' in the title refers to the people. The familial relationships shown in the novel are of two types: That of one's own family and parents and the family of in-laws. The second category applies to Monisha, who is married to a middle-class bhadra family, socially respectable but a plebean family. Monisha is once again an ill-matched character. She is the intellectual type who carries her personal library to her in-laws place contains no light reading or pulp literature but only serious books. However nobody in the family bothers about the books Monisha has in her library. The husband is too busy with his middle rank government job and has no time for his wife. He never shares her feelings. He is another Gautam *(Cry the Peacock)* although less vocal. He is so much under the influence of his family that when once some money is found missing from his pocket he never bothers to ask his wife about it and feels that she has stolen it. The other women in the family are pedestrial, preoccupied with common womanly things like sarees, jewellery and children. Another misfortune of Monisha is that she is sterile. She craves for privacy and even though she has her own room yet it is no more her's, it is always crowded with women and girls of the family :

''Alone, I could work better, and I should feel more – whole. But less and less there is privacy. Even my own room, which they regarded at first as still bridal, now no longer is so (the tubes are blocked, it is no good), and sisters-in-law lie across four-poster, discussing my ovaries and theirs. Kalyani Di throws open my wardrobs in order to inspect my sarees... and sees — my books. The whole wardrobe full of books. To my perplexity. She laughs... I see that... there is nothing to laugh

7. M.K. Naik, *A History of Indian English Literature*, New Delhi, Sahitya Akademi, 1982.

> at in Kafka or Hopkins or Dostoevsky or my Russian or French or Sanskrit dictionaries. But I wish that they would leave me alone, sometimes, to read."[8]

Her husband Nirode has disowned his family and doesn't want to use even the family surname. He is the rebel, always critical, almost vitriolic, courting a life of penury and denial. Although he has some affection for Monisha yet he doesn't bother at all about her mother, who after becoming a widow, is well-off and settled in Kalimpong, looking after her estate. We also have suggestion that she is carrying an affair with a retired military officer which makes Nirode very furious. He doesn't even bother to open her letters addressed to him. She repeatedly asks him to give money but he is so stubborn that he never cares for it. His relationship with his mother is one of love-hate. We have veiled suggestions of his mother-fixation and that is why he hates her so strongly. Psychologists tell us that it is a defence-mechanism of the psyche to stop one from committing incest. As a boy he had addored his mother, treating her like a goddess:

> "Like an antique Goddess" reminding him that as a small boy he had fawned at her feet almost grovelling over her long white toes, while she fastened her ear-ring and glanced with the smile of pride from his little bowed back to her reflection in the mirror." (252).

Even when, towards the end of the novel, she arrives at Calcutta air-port to attend the funeral of Monisha who has committed suicide, she still looks beautiful. He is spell bound by her charms :

> "Still beautiful. And her beauty compelled him to embrace her. The stately and precise figure... (from whom) he could not take his eyes off or, he watched her, petrified, as she came up with her exact and measured walk straight towards him, she stops, stood out as a work of art in crowded, stuffy gallery" (*VC*, pp. 252-53).

Another important novel from the point of view of familial relationship is *Clear Light of Day*. This is a novel about the Das family consisting of the parents, Raja, Baba, a mentally retarded boy, the eldest sister Bim, the younger Tara and a distant poor relative, Mira Masi. The novel covers long span of time covering both British India, and post-independence India. Mr. Das a well-off cultured officer of an insurance company dies prematurely of heart-attack. But his death doesn't really matter because he hardly gave any time to children. During his life time he passed his

8. Anita Desai, *Voices in the City*, Delhi, Orient Paperbacks, 1965.

days in the office, evenings at the club. After his death, being the eldest member of the family, Bim assumes the role of a father, taking care of brothers and sisters and later marrying them. She is so preoccupied with family responsibilities that she has no time for her own love and life. Even though she has an affair with a doctor who becomes her family doctor and it appears that they would be engaged yet somehow things do not happen that way. The irony of the novel is that in spite of her sacrifice at the familial altar everyone is busy in his or her family and she gets nothing but acrimony and bitterness. In the present novel she is a middle aged woman teaching history in a college, living an ascetic life, the only luxury she affords is to buy books. Being deprived of warmth of human relationship or familial relationship books are her only solace and refuge. It is interesting to note that the novel has two epigraphs one by Emily Dicknson and another by T.S. Eliot and in the novel itself there are quotations from English and Urdu poets ranging from Tennyson, Byron, Swinburne, T.S. Eliot and Iqbal. In the context of the present novel this is an important technique used besides flashback and, to some extent, resembles the stream of consciousness technique. Verses quoted in this manner throw light on them and underline suggestiveness of the story.

This device has also been used in *Where Shall We Go This Summer* where Desai quotes a Greek poet and D.H. Lawrence. This is an important device in the sense that poetry is much suggestive and a few lines of a good poem may convey more than several pages of prose. The novel ends with a singer singing a song which provides an insight and a vision, *i.e.* Clear Light of Day. It is a kind of mystic union with him. Besides this song we have quotations from T.S. Eliot's *Four Quartets*, "time the destroyer is time the preserver." But the greater wisdom comes from the lines of Iqbal being sung by the Guru :

> "Your world is the world of fish and fowl my world is the cry at dawn,
> —In your world I am subjected and constrained but over my world you have dominion" (*CLD*, pp. 182-83).

This is the vision that we get from the novel. When familial relationships fail, what works is our relationship with him.

To conclude, from the above thematic survey of some of Anita Desai's novels we find that family and familial relationships play important parts in her fictional world. But what is remarkable is that more often than not the familial relationships are not harmonious. We cannot find a single family in any of her novels which can be called good, if not perfect. This implies that she writes realistic novels and though in the world the institution of family continues to exist yet we seldom find a harmonious family. One may do well with friends or non-familial relationships. But we are at daggers drawn with our own flesh and blood relationships. We cannot choose our relatives but we can certainly choose our friends. But this is the way of the world and none can help it. We have to accept familial relationships whether good or bad.

Chapter IV

AS A SOCIAL BEING

Anita Desai is a mastercrafts woman in situating characters in a particular social set up and valuing him/her in the light of the whole network of relationships that he/shc finds intangled in. The individual is cross referred by polysmic social forces. Society consists of individuals and the individual is a part of society. It is a different matter that some individuals do not go well with the society for a number of reasons. On the one extreme is the Sanyasi who renounces the rules of society. In between comes social reforms, religious leaders and political leaders who rebel against perverted social values and customs in order to make society better. To this group also belongs the artist who carries with him the conventional image of a rebel and that is why in Plato's ideal state as described in *The Republic* there is no place for a poet who is a "liar". In the late 60s and early 70s the phenomenon of Hippy movement was also something similar. There are writers who uphold accepted social values in their fiction creating conformists. But there is also a group of writers who are non-conformists whose characters do not conform to social values. Anita Desai is one of those writers who are more interested in creating characters who are "Nay-Sayers". Speaking about the two kinds of characters who can be described as Aye-Sayers and Nay-Sayers, she has said:

> "There are those who can handle situations and those who can't. "And my stories are generally about those who cannot. They find themselves trapped in situation over which they have no control."[1]

And in support of her above view, she has quoted the following lines from the poem by C.P. Cavafy in *"Where Shall We Go This Summer"*?

> "To certain people there comes a day When they must say the great

---

1. Madhushree Sinha Rao, "Silent Spaces of Inner Vastness," *Times of India*, Delhi, 18.06.1992.

> Yes or the great No. He who has the 'Yes' ready within him reveals himself at once, and saying it crosses over to the path of honour and his own conviction.... He who refuses does not repent. Should he be asked again, he would say No again. And yet that No — the right No — crushes him for the rest of his life."[2]

Not all – Anita Desai's characters are 'Nay-Sayers' but

One may be unhappy with society but there is no escape from society. One may fight with society but one will always remain a part of it.

Nirode in *Voices in the City* is a classic example of the stereotyped majority which is externally critical of and dissatisfied with society.

His deliberate courting of self-denial and poverty is an example of this stubbornness and rebelliousness. Even for meals he goes to his friends:

> "For meals – I scrounge off friends. It's amazing how many willing victims we parasites find ourselves. Society must have some kind of guilt complex about us after all. As for clothes, I haven't needed any for a long time now."[3]

The novel has also been studied from the point of view of existentialism and Nirode quotes Camus, the famous French writer of Existentialist who wrote *The Outsider*. Nirode considers himself an outsider and calls himself "an out-lawed hermit crab."

In his case we can't say that he is a good social being but certainly a social being he is, because, in spite of his bitter criticism of society, he is very much in it and without doing any good to society he lives on it. As quoted above he acknowledges that he is a parasite. He may talk of high things and despise ordinary human beings but he is an unscrupulous man, a cheat, as for some time he makes money by selling fake antique art pieces, for example, a fake bronze depicting :

> "Shiva and Parvati locked together in an upright embrace that pulsed with so grand a desire, so rich a satisfaction that soon the girls, too, looked away from that inscrutable smile on Shiva's face and the taut buttocks of Parvati who had turned her back on the world as she pressed upon her consort her purpose and her delight, inexplicable to both the girls" (*VC*, p. 147).

---

2. Anita Desai, *Where Shall We Go This Summer?* Delhi, Orient Paperbacks, 1982, p. 139. All further references to the novel shall be incorporated in the text.

3. Anita Desai, *Voices in the City*, Delhi, Orient Paperbacks, 1965, p. 59. All further references to the novel shall be incorporated in the text. Henceforth the novel is referred to in the abbreviated form *VC*.

We are later informed that the statue was made by a dubious friend of Nirode "and buried underground for three weeks to give it the appearance of three centuries age" (*VC,* p. 148).

Nirode's sister Monisha is placed in such a bad situation that ultimately she commits suicide. Her's is a case of ill-matched marriage and because of her sensitive character she fails to adjust herself to the suffocating atmosphere of joint family of her in-laws and the result is an unhappy end by burning herself. Women as daughters-in-law in a typical middle class Indian family are not all happy social being. All her ambitions, talent and potentialities are reduced to be a mere housewife and she can do nothing beyond mundane household chores. Anita Desai has very effectively described the position of a *bahu*, caged inside the house. The description comes from Monisha's diary :

> "... . I think of generations of Bengali women hidden behind the barred windows of half-dark rooms, spending centuries in washing clothes, kneading dough and murmuring aloud verses from the *Bhagvad Gita* and the *Ramayana*, in the dim light of sooty lamps. Lives spent in waiting for nothing, waiting on men self-centred and indifferent and hungry and demanding and critical, waiting for death and dying misunderstood, always behind bars, those terrifying black bars that shut us in, in the old city ... . The eyes of these silent Bengali women are not dead, but they anticipate death, as they do everything with resignation. There is no dignity in their death as in the death of that proud and glorious beast, but only a little melancholy as in the settling of a puff of dust upon the earth..." (*VC,* pp. 120-121).

Besides the above two major characters another character is an artist named Dharma with whom Nirode's other sister Amla falls in love. Amla is an artist who has come from Bombay after studying commercial art and has come to Calcutta to make her professional career. Nirode true to his bitter and cynical temperament disapproves of the very idea of commercial art: "Commercial artist, sounds too bloody and full for words. Poor old Amla do you really expect anything from a career stamped commercial?" (*VC,* p. 154).

Dharma is a friend of Nirode. His daughter had eloped with her cousin and in order to avoid humiliation from society he had left Calcutta and settled down in the suburb. Amla has a passing affair with Dharma but realising that love with a married person will lead to a dead end she leaves him. Amla's mind is haunted by some questions regarding Dharma and society. It is because of his unhappy experience that Dharma has turned into a bitter man. His daughter had eloped with her first cousin,

Dharma's sister's son, "a boy whom I had brought up as her brother" (*VC*, p. 228).

Amla wonders what Dharma hated in society: "What was it in society he truly hated – the rules and restrictions that he verbally opposed, or their transgression that is secretly feared and loathed?" (*VC*, p. 228). As is the case of Monisha Dharma's marriage is also not a happy one. Marriage being an important social institution is a part of one's social being. In the novel we come across two observations on marriage and both of them are derogatory.

In the first instance it comes from Nirode when he visits his friend Jit:

> "Marriage, bodies, touch and torture... he shuddered and, walking swiftly, was almost afraid of the dark of Calcutta, its warmth that clung to one with a moist, perspiring embrace, rich with the odours of open gutters and tuberose, garlands. All that was Jit's and Sarla's, he decided, and indeed all that had to do with marriage, was destructive, negative,decadent. He could waste no time on it..." (*VC*, p. 35).

The second observation comes from Dharma. When Amla asks about his wife's sympathy with him or the daughter who had run away, this is what Dharma says and what he says is certainly not in praise of marriage:

> "Our relationship is not all so straightforward and pat, married relationships never are. There is the matter of loyalty, habit, complicity – things I couldn't talk to you about till you married and knew for yourself (*VC*, p. 229).

These character studies from *Voices in the City* present different types of social beings but all of them appear to be socially maladjusted. Most of Anita Desai's novels deal with such characters and the reasons for their maladjustment vary from character to character. In Nirode's case it is because of his high-brow attitude, in Monisha's because of her sensitivity, and in Dharma's case because of his artistic preoccupation and personal tragedy in his life.

In Custody is a novel about an unheroic, unimpressive and unassertive lecturer of Hindi in a mofussil Degree College near Delhi, named Deven who is married to an insipid wife Sarla who is miles away from her husband's literary taste and intellectual pursuit. He is an Urdu enthusiast and wants to interview an established ageing poet of Urdu with two wives. The whole novel is about the interview which is beset with many obstacles and mishaps and when at long last it materialises the tape recorder is not operated well and what is recorded is a string of nonsense utterances of the senile poet blabbering about *biryani*, pigeon fight, wrestling bouts and memories of his young days. Since the interview was financed by a grant from the college the tape of the interview was to be deposited in the college. But what was there on the tape worth depositing? Deven is in a plight and he does not know what to do. He is so much enamoured of the personality of the poet that he seems to be in custody of the poet.

Deven's social role is that of a teacher but because of his poor personality he commands no respect from his students. While taking class instead of looking at the students he would be looking outside the class towards an imaginary audience. No wonder he was an unsuccessful teacher "who could not command attention, let alone the regard of his unruly class."[4] The students are rowdy and take no interest in studies. Deven in quite opposite of the traditional image of a Guru. He is always unsure of himself and because of his simplicity and tactlessness bordering on being a simpleton he always lands in some odd situation.

His unsympathetic and un-understanding wife has absolutely no idea about her husband's preoccupation and suspects that his frequent trips to Delhi are in order to meet his girl-friend. Whereas the fact is that Deven is so timid that he can hardly make friends with any girl. Sarla the wife knows nothing but to fret and sulk leading a dry existence always cross with her husband. Financially not well-off, Deven's marital life is insipid. Sarla tries to discharge her duties as a housewife but there is nothing attractive either about her body or her temperament. Deven's preoccupation with his literary pursuit and supercillious attitude towards his wife makes things even worse. Once again it is an ill-matched marriage which is a favourite theme of Anita Desai. Deven's two aspects of his social being are as husband and as teacher and he is a failure in both of them.

Political system and values are also part of society and one's social being includes them also. In the present novel although politics does not figure directly yet political views indirectly affect the life of Deven. The language controversy of Hindi and Urdu is referred to in the novel. The two camps of Hindi and Urdu are represented respectively by Trivedi, the Head of the Hindi Department in Deven's college and Nur, the Urdu poet. It is ironical that Deven's enthusiasm and love for Urdu literature is misunderstood by Trivedi who is a staunch Hindiwalla and on political front who can be a better advocate of Rashtrabhasha than the R.S.S.

Trivedi dislikes Deven's interest in Urdu and this dislike comes

4. Anita Desai, *In Custody*, London, William Heinemann Limited, 1984, p. 13. All subsequent references will be incorporated in the text. Henceforth the novel is referred to in the abbreviated form *IC*.

openly when he goes to him for asking for one week's leave to go to Delhi to interview the poet:

> 'One week? It would be a relief to me if it were one year,' bawled Trivedi, 'and I did not need to see your stupid mug again. I'll have you demoted, Sharma — I'll see to it you don't get your confirmation. I'll get you transferred to your beloved Urdu department. I won't have Muslim toadies in my department, you'll ruin my boys with your Muslim ideas, your Urdu language. I'll complain to the Principal, I'll warn the R.S.S. you are a traitor...' (*IC*).

The language controversy and the conflict between Hindi and Urdu have received attention in the novel. Language is a tool of society primarily to communicate but as civilisation goes language becomes a powerful medium not only for expression of culture in the form of literature but also for expressing the national the socio-cultural identity of a nation. In its positive aspects language is perhaps the greatest achievement of the human being, the medium in which a nation's cultural heritage is preserved and passed on to posterity. But in its negative aspects language may play havoc with nations specially in a country like India which has multilinguistic groups. All of us are familiar with the conflict centering around the issue of national language and how periodically language riots in the South destroy huge amount of public property. Language is not merely a scientific set of rules with a vocabulary to be handled coldly by computers but it is deeply rooted in our psyche exercising powerful influence on our sentiments. Since language is a part of society therefore it is also an inalienable part of our social being. Language controversy and its socio-cultural and political implications and effects are not only peculiar to India but can also be seen in countries like Canada. But there it is only a matter of two languages, English and French, whereas in India there are thirteen languages recognised by the Constitution. Mercifully all of them do not have enough political pressure to build up a situation of civil disturbances.

In the context of the novel Deven the unheroic hero, is caught between two languages, Hindi which is the source of his livelihood and Urdu which he loves. The Urdu supporters vomit out all their hatred against Hindi, Murad is one of them who brings out an Urdu magazine for which he commissions Deven to take interview of Nur. He worries about the dwindling number of Urdu readers :

> Worries, worries, worries. And where are the readers? Where are the subscriptions? Who reads Urdu any more? (*IC*, p. 15).

He considers himself a patron and a well-wisher of Urdu language and feels great pride in saying that he is trying to keep alive the delicate language. But that is not enough. In order to establish the superiority of the Urdu language as though he must denigrate Hindi:

> "Now I am planning, a special issue on Urdu poetry. Someone has to keep alive the glorious tradition of Urdu literature. If we do not do it, at whatever cost, how will it survive in this era of — that vegetarian monster, Hindi?.... 'That language of peasants,'.... 'The language that is raised on radishes and potatoes,'.... Yet, like these vegetables, it flourishes, while Urdu – the language of the court in days of royalty — now languishes in the back lanes and gutters of the city. No palace for it to live in the style of which it is accustomed, no emperors and nawabs to act as its patrons. Only poor I, in my dingy office, trying to bring out a magazine where it may be kept alive. That is what I am doing, see?" (*IC,* p. 15).

Murad has a self-congratulatory attitude towards Urdu. Nur has another attitude towards the language and he gives absolutely no credit to academies for the well-being of the language. He is so disgusted with the universities that he calls them graveyards of the language. The occasion for his outburst is a gathering of young poets who are reciting their poems in *tarannum* at Nur's house :

> 'Cowards — babies...' You recite verses as if they were nursery rhymes your mother had composed. I tell you, we must get over this rolling of Urdu verses into little sugar pills for babies to suck. We need the roar of lions, or the boom of cannon, so that we can march upon these Hindi-wallahs and make them run. Let them see the power of Urdu, he thundered. 'They think it is chained and tamed in the dusty yards of those cemetries that they call universities, but can't we show them that it can still let out a roar or a boom?'.... Yes, let Urdu issue from any orifice as long as it drives them away. But make its presence felt, 'he thundered thumping down his glass on his knee so that the liquor flew from it' (*IC,* pp. 52-53).

A more rational approach comes from another man who may have been a journalist :

> "Nur Sahib, I am telling you the time for poetry is over. To feed the Hindi-wallahs with Urdu poetry is like feeding cows with—hunks of red meat. Turn to journalism instead, Nur Sahib. Reach out to the people directly. We have a message for them. Tell them in plain speech. Use your powers for the purpose of — attack and vengeance!" (*IC,* p . 53).

Since the two languages belong to two different and hostile religions the language issue is politicised and it is this political angle that Deven dislikes and avoids, "He had always kept away from the political angle of languages. He began to sweat with fear" (*IC,* p. 55). In the gathering at Nur's house there are also Hindi supporters who speak in praise of Hindi, "Vegetarian Hindi". Anita Desai perceptually observes that language issue has vitiated the mind of the intelligentsia evoking from it stereotype responses and argument. Such debates are inconclusive "as the rice and gravy live on trays all over the terrace." This is how the language issue and its controversies are described :

> "There was the India camp and the Pakistan camp, the pure-Persian camp and the demotic-Hindustani camp. They quarrelled and mocked and taunted and lost their tempers, but as if acting assigned roles. There was no evidence of anyone persecuting anyone else or of winning anyone over to his side through argument of persuasion" (*IC,* p. 54).

Nur is as contemptuous of Hindi as Murad. He taunts Deven and asks him to forget about Urdu literature and his poetry and go back to his college and "... teach your students the stories of Prem Chand, the poems of Pant and Nirala. Save, simple Hindi language, save comfortable ideas of cow worship and caste and the romance of Krishna" (*IC,* p. 55).

According to Nur Urdu died in 1947 when the country become independent. But the fact is that even today government of India is running University Departments of Urdu, *Madarasas* and Urdu academies. But throughout the novel the Urdu-walla projected that Urdu was hardly beyond being a court language in Moghal Empire. The court language had always been Persian and Urdu was a language of soldiers; the literal meaning of Urdu is tent where soldiers live. Even the late 19th century Urdu poets like Ghalib and Meer wrote much of their poetry in Persian.

Since language is politicised so it is bound to have effects on society and this comes in the form of communal riots. In the novel we have reference to it. In *Baumgartner's Bombay* we find communal riot but it was post-partition riot in Calcutta. But in this novel it seems to be of recent times:

> "Naturally the area around the mosque was considered the 'Muslim' area, and the rest 'Hindu'. This was not strictly so and there were certainly no boundaries or demarcations, ...so that pigs were generally kept out of the vicinity of the mosque and cows never slaughtered near a temple. Once a year, during the Mohurram procession of *tazias* through the city, police sprang up everywhere with batons,

sweating with a sense of responsibility and heightened tension, intent on keeping the processions away from the temples and from hordes of homeless cows or from groups of gaily coloured citizens who unfortunately often celebrated Holi with packets of powdered colours and buckets of coloured water on the same day as that of the ritual mourning. If these clashed, as happened from time to time, knives flashed, batons failed and blood ran. For a while tension was high, the newspapers — both in Hindi and Urdu — were filled with guarded reports and fulsome editorials on India's secularity while overnight news sheets appeared with less guarded reports laced with threats and accusations'' (*IC*, p. 21).

Thus we find that *In Custody* is a novel that presents several aspects of society and tells us how Deven has to carry himself as a social being. His position is not very happy but through him we come across different kinds of people representing different social classes, a wide range of teachers, shopkeepers, the poet and his hangers-on, and students. It is mainly through Deven that the story has been narrated and mainly it is through him that the theme of man as a social being is expressed in the novel.

As said earlier Anita Desai specialises in creating the 'Nay-sayers' in her novels and such characters are bound to come in conflict with society. They do not fit smugly in the socially allotted slots, they are no mere cogs in the machinery called society. Thus they are misfits as social beings. There is a host of such characters and Nirode in *Voices in the City* is its classic example. One's personality and life is most affected when society imposes certain norms on the characters and demands conformity to them and when they don't conform society ostracises them and demands a pound of flesh. Monisha from the same novel is another example of such a non-conformist. The tension between her individual being and several other beings is so great that she breaks down, pushed to the wall and being a sensitive woman she is compelled to commit suicide. Society is an abstract concept and hence it operates through the members of society, be they husbands and in-laws or other persons. Society exercises its influence and control on the individual through social values. And when those values are perverted the influence becomes suffocating and life-sucking, making the individual a psychological cripple living in the hinterland of reality and fantasy. Anita Desai is not merely a domestic novelist writing about family and man-woman relationship but at times goes beyond the limits of family exploring and portrayal of social prejudices and perverted social values that affect the individual.

There may be various kinds of such social biases and values that affect the individual. They may be communal or socio-political.

Baumgartner's Bombay and *Bye-Bye Black Bird* are two novels in which perverted socio-political and communal values or biases make the life of the individual a hell. In both these novels there is xenophobia or dislike for the foreigners. First we would take up *Bye-Bye Black Bird* which has an international theme in the sense that Adit marries an English girl Sarah and by doing so he incurs the anger of the white society. Ironically, it is not Adit who suffers most on this account but his docile wife Sarah. By marrying a brown Asian she has broken the social code of England hence she is always subject to taunts and jibes of not only her colleagues but even of young pupils of the school where she works as a clerk. She always avoids any question regarding her husband and family life but her peers take a perverse delight in asking such questions. Julia who is a teacher in her school comes out with typical British superciliousness. Sarah dreads such embarrassing comments:

> "She was still breathing hard at having so narrowly escaped having to answer personal questions. It would have wrecked her for the whole day to have to discuss Adit with Julia, with Miss Pimm, in this sane, chalk-dusted, work-a-day office. She was willing to listen for hours to Miss Pimm's diagnosis of her aches and pains." "... .But to display her letters from India, to discuss her Indian husband, would have forced her to parade like an impostor, to make claims to a life, an identity that she did not herself feel to be her own, although they would have been more than ready to believe her." "... She had stammered out her replies, too unhappy even to accuse them of tactlessness or inquisitiveness and, for her pains, had heard Julia sniff, as she left the room, "If she's ashamed of having an Indian husband, why did she go and marry him?"[5]

What of grown-ups, even the young ones emulating the elders taunt her. Her pupils ignore her and taunt. As she darted through their throng, they pretended not to notice her at all, but once she came across the road, she heard them scream, "Hurry hurry, Mrs. *Scurry*!" And "Where's the fire, pussy cat?" (*BBBB*, p. 32). This much about the ordeal she undergoes at her work place at the hands of her colleagues and pupils. But the strains of inter-racial marriage are so much on her that they affect her day-to-day life. When she goes for shopping she avoids going to the stores of Laurel

5. Anita Desai, *Bye-Bye Black Bird*, Delhi, Orient Paperbacks, 1985, p. 36-37. All further references to the novel shall be incorporated in the text. Henceforth the novel is referred to in the abbreviated form *BBBB*.

Lane where she lives, for her shopping would easily betray her link with India. So she prefers going to big department store where she would remain an anonymous buyer, none knowing her Asian connections:

> "...she went into the supermarket to wander amongst the stacked shelves in an absent-mindedly happy way for she loved the supermarket, only just remembering to snatch up a bottle of mango chutney and a Lyons blackberry pie in order not to arouse the accountant's suspicion. The supermarket was a soothing place to her. Here she could buy her Patna rice and her pickles without acquiring the distinct personality; these purchases would have marked her with, had she shopped for them in one of those pleasant little shops at the end of Laurel Lane,"
> "... . But inside the sparkling halls of the supermarket where walls of soap and cornflakes hid her from strangers' eyes, she could be as eccentric, as individual, as she pleased without being noticed by even a mouse" (*BBBB,* pp. 38-39).

But in spite of all her precautions she cannot escape the charade which is now part of her life. The tension between pretension and actuality, appearance and reality is always there which tells upon her, resulting in schizophrenia: She does not know to where she belongs and she is fed up with putting on faces. She wants genuineness and that would come only when she leaves England for good at the end of the novel. We are not told how she would fare in the Indian society but from the internal evidence of the novel it is suggested that she would be accepted by her Indian in-laws. In England she is not at peace. Her identity crisis has been described more than once in the novel which makes her lonely, the question always nagging her who is she. Here are two examples from chapter II of the novel. After marriage she faces an identity crisis :

> "She had become nameless, she had shed her name as she had shed her ancestry and identity, and she sat there, staring, as though she watched them disappear. Or could only someone who knew her, knew of her background and her marriage, imagine this? Would a stranger have seen in her a lost maiden in search of her name that she seemed, with a sudden silver falling of the light of glamour, to an unusually subdued and thoughtful Adit?" (*BBBB,* p. 31).

A clearer description of Sarah's identity crisis is to be found in a later authorial comment in the same chapter of the novel. If a girl marries in the same culture it is easier for her to adjust to her new home and people. But inter-racial and inter-cultural marriage causes adjustment problems which are not easy to overcome. In Sarah's case the problem becomes more complicated for she has married a person whose race was once ruled over by her own in spite of 'progress' and 'modernity' old prejudices die hard. Sarah is homeless in her own native country which is the biggest irony. The question continues to nag her, Who was she?

> "Who was she – Mrs. Sen who had been married in a red and gold Benares brocade saree one burning, bronzed day in September, or Mrs. Sen, the Head's secretary, who sent out the bills and took in the cheques, kept order in the school and was known for her efficiency? Both these creatures were frauds, each had a large, shadowed element of charade about it. When she briskly dealt with letters." "...she felt an impostor, but, equally, she was playing a part when she tapped her fingers to the sitar music on Adit's records." ".... She had so little command over these two charades she played each day, one in the morning at school and one in the evening at home, that she could not ever tell with how much sincerity she played one role or the other. They were roles and when she was not playing them, she was nobody. Her face was only a mask, her body only a castume. Where was Sarah?" "...she wondered if Sarah had any existence at all, and then she wondered, with great sadness, if she would ever be allowed to step off the stage, leave the theatre and enter the real world — whether English or Indian, she did not care, she wanted only its sincerity, its truth" (*BBBB,* pp. 34-35).

Sarah's problem is human. She wants to be a real person whether English or Indian. She is fed up with sitting on the fence.

She tries her best to remain a sincere wife seeing to it that her marital life is not destroyed. Her husband too had been playing charade although not as consciously as she. But he also realises falseness of his existence in England and Sarah also knows it full well: "His whole personality seemed to her to have cracked apart into an unbearable number of disjointed pieces, rattling together noisily and disharmoniously" (*BBBB,* p. 200). When after the 1965 Indo-Pak war Adit is in the process of making a decision to leave England for good, he is very edgy and unstable and this is the time when he needs a cooperative understanding wife. And Sarah does well as the wife. Of all wives of Anita Desai she is the best in understanding and supports her husband. In the circumstance mentioned above she knows how to handle her husband :

> "She could not tell what effect the smallest refusal or contradiction might have on him.... Rather she would sacrifice anything, anything at all, in order to maintain, however superficially, a semblance of order and discipline in her house, in her relationship with him. His

whole personality seemed to her to have cracked apart,... . If she allowed this chaos to reflect upon their marriage, she knew its fragments would not remain jangling together but would scatter, drift and crumble'' (*BBBB*, p. 200).

The above study of the novel shows that even though socially Sarah is not very happy because of racial prejudice of her people yet as a wife she very sensibly takes care of things. Most of Anita Desai's couples don't pull well in marriage but happily here we have a warm understanding wife that is Sarah. Her social being may not be satisfied and contented but her familial being, which is much more important for one's happiness, is contented. We have all our praise for this alien woman who understands her husband, his family and country which she would accept, once in India. And the novel ends with their departure to India bidding goodbye: *Bye-Bye Black Bird.*

Anita Desai's latest novel *Baumgartner's Bombay* (1988) too has for its theme the individual in relation to society or to be more accurate the individual as a product of society. Once again we have tension between the individual and the social forces or perverted social values. The novel covers both Europe and India. It is the study of an uprooted Jew, Victor Baumgartner, who is persecuted in his own country because of perverse Nazi anti-semitism, too dark to be accepted in his own country and before the Second Wold War when he comes to the British India in search of a better future he is too fair-skinned to be accepted by the Indian society. Here he is considered a *firangi* and *mleccha*. In this novel the racial feeling is even more telling and touching than in *Bye-Bye Black Bird.* Baumgartner's is a very human tragedy. He is not accepted anywhere, neither in his country of birth, Nazi Germany, nor in his adopted country India. In his own country he is a victim of religious persecution, a factor over which he has no control. It is just a matter of accident of having been born in a Jewish family. His father had a prosperous business of furniture and they were well-off but as Hitler's party came to power and began its death-dance on Jews euphemistically called 'Jewish solution', his father's property was confiscated and he was asked to try his luck in British India. He arrives in Bombay and then goes to Calcutta to do business in timber. For sometimes things go well and then the Second World War breaks out and he along with many Germans, enemy aliens, is imprisoned. It is ironical that he is clubbed with Germans whom he hates.

Before the outbreak of the war he is taken to be a British by Calcuttans. When he goes to buy cigarettes he is accosted by street-walkers, prostitutes, who take him to be a Tommy. It is a comic situation.

He does not want these stinking prostitutes:

> "Going out for a packet of cigarettes from a stall he had noticed at the corner, late at night when the shops were shut, he was hailed by two women who stood by a high wall that stank of urine and garbage. They wore white frocks, like nurses, and jewellery of glass, and tin. When they smiled at him, waving 'Hoo-hoo, Tommy,' he saw that their teeth were stained red, ... they grabbed him by an arm each, crying, 'Less have drink, Tommy, come *awn.*' ...they smelt of Eastern flowers — jasmine, or lotus, as well as perspiration, cheap cigarettes, alcohol and the stuff they chewed with their strong, flashing teeth, spitting frequently to rid their mouths of its crimson juice."[6]

Baumgartner's long detention in prison camp is another aspect of his social being, a role he is compelled to play. The British think, since he is a German passport holder, that he is an enemy. They can hardly appreciate that his race is persecuted by the Germans. When he tries to explain to a British officer that he is a refugee in this country and happens to be a German passport holder, he is snubbed :

> "What am I to do then?" The man bawled when Baumgartner again protested at being labelled a German and 'hostile'. 'Got a German passport, says you were born there – then what am I supposed to take you for, a bloomin Indian?' The papers were flung at him, and he retreated, baffled, wondering what magic word he might find that would release him from what was a monstrous mistake, or madness" (*BB,* p. 106).

The greatest humiliation and chagrin he experiences when in the prison camp he is compelled by some Nazi Germans to sing song for Nazis. This is the nadir of Baumgartner's role as a social being described in an ironical and touchingly human way :

> "... the song of graves and funerals, of death on battlefields, of endings and defeats":
>
> *'Ich hat' ein Kamerad,*
>
> *Einen bessern find'st due night ...'*
>
> "The men in the audience gave a collective shiver." "... Baumgartner stood, under the weight of their defeat, burdened by their defeat,

6. Anita Desai, *Baumgartner's Bombay*, London, William Heinemann Limited, 1988, p. 92. All further references to the novel shall be incorporated in the text in abbreviated form as *BB*.

finding it gross, grotesque, suffocating. He wanted to say 'Stop!' He wanted to tell them it was their defeat, not his, that their country might be destroyed but this meant a victory, terribly late, far too late, but at last the victory. Of course he said nothing, he stood helplessly, only aware how crushed and wretched a representative he was of victory. Couldn't even victory appear in colours other than that of defeat? No. Defeat was heaped on him, whether he deserved it or not'' (*BB*, p. 135).

This is a bad kind of social pressure coming on to Baumgartner from his peer group. But still worse things are to come. We have seen in an earlier chapter how Lotte had been shunned by Kanti Sethia's family. In Baumgartner's case too such shocks are in store. After the end of the war came India's independence and partition and attendant massive communal riots. Peace loving Baumgartner is never at peace. When he goes to Calcutta it is the city in flame engulfed by communal riots, arson and murders. This time violence and destruction are before his eyes — senseless, insane, violence and killing. Baumgartner's business associate, a Muslim is missing. Unlike the Second World War fought in far off in Europe and Far East, communal war is right in front of him in Calcutta. When released from the prison, Baumgartner comes back to the city where he had enjoyed peace and life :

> ''Baumgartner felt himself overtaken by yet another war of yet another people. Done with the global war, only to be plunged into a religious war. Endless war. Eternal war. Twenty thousand people, the newspapers informed him, were killed in three days of violence in Calcutta. Muslims killed Hindus, Hindus, Muslims. Baumgartner could not fathom it — to him they were Indians seen in a mass and, individually, Sushil the Marxist, Habibullah the trader'' (*BB*, p. 180).

It is ironical that Baumgartner himself, being a Jew, should know about inter-religious hatred between them and Christians, hostility that goes back to history and examples of Jew-hatred can be seen in writers like Marlowe, Shakespeare, and John Galsworthy.

Baumgartner's tragedy is his homelessness and rootlessness. We have seen how he is thrown out of his fatherland. In India he wants to be accepted but because of his colour he is not to be taken as a native. That is his dilemma. To some extent his plight is similar to that of Joe Christmas in William Faulkner's *Light in August*. In India he is taken as an outsider, *firangi* and *mleccha*. His colour betrays his identity. We wished he could be darker but ''Daily he grew redder. Would he one day be darker? It seemed desperately important to belong and to make a place for himself''(*BB*, p. 93). His colour is a handicap in his human relationship, *e.g.* his friendship with Chaman Lal. When his best friend Chaman Lal collapses at the race course in Baumgartner's lap he proves to be a good friend, taking him to the hospital. But he dies and when he goes to attènd his funeral he can easily see that Chamanlal's relatives are resenting his presence. It is touching that he cannot even attend the last rites of his best friend, which serves as an example of perverted social value :

> ''Baumgartner joined the mourners at the cremation, standing at the edge of the crowd, all of whom shark away from him, horrified by the presence of a foreigner, a *firangi*, at such an intensely private rite. Hearing the babbling chant of the odours of burnt flesh and charred wood under the noontime sun, Baumgartner too wished he had not come, and shuffled away'' (*BB*, pp. 205-206).

This rejection of Baumgartner is similar to that of Kantibhai's family's rejection of Lotte. Indians behave with them in an unjust biased manner. Baumgartner does not want anything from Chamanlal's family. He only wants acceptance and affection. He wants human relationship with them. But it is not to be. Even after living for fifty long years in India, he finds himself an alien. His own country has no attraction for him. Once talking with Lotte he says Germany has nothing for people like them. He has no other way out to accept India as his country. He does it out of compulsion for, there is nothing for him in Germany. He realises it even earlier in the prison camp. He is musing about his long internment and its effect on him and more importantly what would he do once he is free :

> ''He wondered if the long internment had not incapacitated him, made him unfit for the outer world. And what would they find outside? Germany destroyed — no possibility of returning, so that he would have to accept India as his permanent residence. He wondered at his ability to survive in it, reduced as he was to such an abject state of helplessness, and the knowledge besides of being alone.'' ''... Outside, he would be that — a man without a family or a country'' (*BB*, pp. 132-133).

Baumgartner's tragedy is very near us today when several countries are engulfed in civil war, be it Bosnia or Somalia or Burgundy. Wars are fought by politicians, tribal leaders or military junta but it is the ordinary man who suffers. But those in power have no feeling for the ordinary man. Baumgartner is not only the victim of political power but more so of perverted social values and biased attitude. After the war things should improve, but they do not. Once he suffered at the hands of Nazis then the British and in the end in independent India. He fails to understand why

Indian people don't accept him. Certain individuals do accept him, but not society at large. Simple man that he is, he fails to comprehend the reason. He muses, and broods:

> "He had lived in this land for fifty years — or if not fifty then so nearly as to make no difference — and it no longer seemed fantastic and exotic; it was more utterly familiar now than any other landscape on earth. Yet in the eyes of the people he was still strange and unfamiliar to them, and all said: *Firangi*, foreigner. For the Indian sun had not been good to his skin, it had not tanned and roasted him to the colour of a native." "... His hair would not turn dark; it stood out around the bald centre like a white ruff, stained somewhat yellow. Even if he had used hair-dye and bootpolish, what could he have done about his eyes? It was not that they were blue — far from it; his mother, holding him on her knee... had called them 'dark eyes, *dunkele Augen,*' but Indians did not seem to think them so. Their faces sneered '*firangi,* foreigner,' however good-naturedly, however lacking in malice." "... Accepting but not accepted; that was the story of his life, the one thread that ran through it all. In Germany he had been dark — his darkness had marked him the Jew, *der Jude*. In India he was fair — and that marked him the *firangi*. In both lands, the unacceptable. Perhaps even where his cats were concerned, he was that – man, not feline, not theirs. He nodded thoughtfully; *ja*, the cats, they always knew" (*BB,* pp. 19-20).

Thus we find that Baumgartner accepts Indian society, but he is not accepted by it. In the course of the novel he plays different social roles but his social being is not satisfactory. He always remains the victim of society, of specific perverted social values, whether in his native country Germany or his adopted country India. Only in British India he is happy but that too not for long. His tragedy has been succinctly summed up in the following quotation : "Accepting but not accepted; that was the story of his life, the one thread that ran through it all."

Chapter V

ANITA DESAI'S FICTIONAL TECHNIQUES

> *When we speak of technique, we speak of nearly everything. For technique is the means by which the writer's experience, which is his subject matter, compels him to attend to it; technique is the only means he has to discovering, exploring, developing his subject, of conveying its meaning, and finally, of evaluating it.... Technique in fiction is, of course, all those obvious forms of it which are usually taken to be the whole of it, and many others... . Technique is really what T.S. Eliot means by "convention'— any selection, structure, or distortion, any form or rhythm imposed upon the world of action; by means of which – it should be added – our apprehension of the world of action is enriched or renewed. In this sense, everything is technique which is not the lump of experience itself, and one cannot properly say that a writer has no technique or that he eschews technique for being a writer, he cannot do so. We can speak of good and bad technique, of adequate and inadequate of technique which serves the novel's purpose, or disserves.*[1]

The word "technique" is devised from the Greek *technikos techni* meaning an art, artifice. The hypothetical Indo-European root of the word is *tekth* — meaning to weave, to build, to join whence the Greek word *takton* meaning a carpenter. Similarly later in Latin *texere* means to weave, to build. Thus the word in its original form meant an applied art whether of building a house or of weaving a piece of cloth. And from usage in such practical art the term was later applied to literature. Literature being a world of imagination has to borrow words from the "practical" world for its uses. As an artisan or a skilled worker uses some

1. Mark Schorer, "Technique as Discovery", See Handy and Westbook (Eds.), *Twentieth Century Criticism : The Major Statements,* New Delhi, Light and Life Publications, 1976, p. 71-72.

tools, methods and devices in producing an object, whether a piece of furniture or a tapestry, similarly a literary artist has to use some tools, devices, and methods in creating a literary work. As mentioned in the epigraph to the chapter above, the word technique in the context of literature has a wide scope of meaning. When a novelist writes a novel he conveys his theme with the help of a story which consists of certain events taking place through certain characters. And since the novel is a verbal form so the story is to be narrated. Narrating a story is a primitive instinct and literature of every language, even the one without script, has a stock of stories transmitted through generations orally. Obviously the narrative method employed therein was crude but narrative it certainly was. Over the years narrative skill or craft of fiction developed. In the late nineteenth century French critic Flanbert gave the famous dictum that "the artist is like God present everywhere but seen no where" which means that in a fictional work since the writer creates character he is omniscient but objectivity and artistic detachment demand that he shouldn't take sides with characters. The other important development was that the narrative should not be disrupted by authorial comment or direct address to the reader, a practice favourite with Victorian novelists and later with an otherwise perfect novelist Thomas Hardy. This dispels the illusion of make-belief or hampers what Coleridge said in a better phrase, willing suspension of disbelief. Generally, the novelist adopts the method of omniscient narrator *i.e.* the novelist knows all, entering in the mind of different characters and revealing their thought process to the reader.

As the epigraphs to the chapter suggests technique in fiction includes almost everything that goes into making the novel. Simplistically speaking, technique includes everything that the novelist uses for narrating his story. On finer level it means imagery, symbolism, point of view, chronological order of events, stream of consciousness, schematisation of chapter division or some other basis of division of the novel, etc. Dialogue, language, characterisation, and plot are some other aspects of fictional technique. Some novelists are deliberately conscious of technique and rely on technical innovations and some are satisfied with the mere basics. We have already studied Anita Desai's themes in preceding chapters, Now we have to study her fictional technique in relation to her different novels. Curiously there is not a large corpus of criticism on her fictional technique and critics have addressed themselves to other aspects of her novels. Perhaps it is because she is not considered a technical innovator but it does not mean that she has no technique. As Mark Schorer has written no writer can be without technique, as no painter can paint without brush and palette, so is the case with Anita Desai. Now we would study Anita Desai's fictional technique by taking each of her novels in chronological order.

Her first novel is *Cry the Peacock* (1962) which is the story of a sensitive, introvert, childless woman haunted by a prophecy made to her during her childhood. The novel begins with an apparently trivial incident of the death of the heroine's pet dog Toto. She being childless was much attached to the dog and his death was a shattering experience for her. But her rational husband cannot appreciate the tragedy. The story is not narrated in straight chronological order. There is a mixture of the past and the present in the narrative. The reader is taken to Maya's childhood experience. Since the prophecy plays an important part in the novel and haunts Maya's mind hence the childhood memory of her going to the temple with her ayah is repeated time and again. The memory of this incident is like a leitmotif in the novel. The prophecy has left such deep impression on the child Maya's mind that it remains vivid even years after the incident :

> ''My child, I would not speak of it if I saw it on your face alone. But look, look at the horoscope. Stars do not lie. And so it is best to warn you, prepare you.'... ! Death,'... 'to one of you. When you are married'...''young''... . 'Death — an early one — by unnatural causes. ... the child must be persuaded, she must listen to my warning. It is my duty to prepare her, my duty.'... . ''Four years after your marriage, so the stars prophecy, and the space between your eyes, the mark there, supports this prophecy I have warned you, performed my duty. Be wary, child, be wary and fear God.''[2]

The recurrence of memory of the incident is a device to show Maya's pre-occupation with the prophecy. Since she belongs to a traditional Brahmin family her faith in astrology is but natural. People all over the world have faith in astrology but in Indian context it becomes all the more important where still in traditional Brahmin families marriage is fixed only after tallying the horoscope. Ascetics may call astrology pseudo science yet in the novel it plays an important role in Maya's character.

Anita Desai creates contrasting characters to highlight the main character. Pom is foil to Maya's character. If Maya is traditional,

2. Anita Desai, *Cry the Peacock*, Delhi, Orient Paperbacks 1980, p. 29-31. All further references to the novel shall be incorporated in the text.

sensitive, refined, Pom has none of these qualities. In her world there is no place for tradition :

> "Logic, tact, diplomacy — nothing mattered to her who chattered so glibly and gaily all the day long, jumping up now and then to bring out a new pair of shoes, a new set of rings to show me, talking with eagerness and animation of anything that was new and bright, and never, never referring to family, tradition, custom, superstition, all that I dreaded now. I was certain she hated such talk as much as I did, even if she had no reason to fear them. Such things simply did not step over the bright enamelled horizon of her painted world, for such things bore shadows, and shadows were alien to her as once, in a similar world, if a richer and more refined one, they had been alien to me, who now constantly looked behind to see where the purple ghost of the albino followed on silk-swathed, oil-softened feet" (*CP*, p. 61).

Similarly Gautam's character is also foil to Maya's. He is rational and quotes the *Bhagwad Gita*. Because of the dissimilar characters they do not pull well. After Toto's death very sensibly he suggests that he will bring another for her. Leila's character is another aspect of fatalism, she has knowingly married a man suffering from T.B. If Maya is moving towards fatalism caused by the prophecy, Leila is already an example of accepting fatalism.

Anita Desai's use of symbolism has evoked critical writings. As the title shows the peacock is an important symbol of the novel. B. Ramchandra Rao[3] finds the dance of peacock as both the dance of life and the dance of death. P.K. Pandey has worked out religio-cultural aspects of the symbol and finds it to be "the central symbol to feminine psyche, having religio-cultural roots that enrich the meaning by providing undertones to the symbol." He also comments on the hundred eyes on the peacock's feather. Maya calls these eyes the eyes of wisdom which is to be seen in relation to eye symbolism, the eye which is window to knowledge. Although Indian goddess of wisdom Saraswati is associated with *Hansa* (goose) yet some Jain work on iconography mentions the peacock as her mount. She is called *Mayur Vahimi*, she who rides a peacock.[4]

Another important symbol used is that of Shiva. B. Ramchandra Rao finds Natraj a symbol of liberation and observes "the Natraj reinforces

3. B. Ramchandra Rao, *The Novels of Mrs. Anita Desai*, Ludhiana, Kalyani Publishers, 1977, p. 17.

4. P.K. Pandeya, "*Feminine Psyche In Cry the Peacock,*" Indian Woman Novelist. Set I, Vol. III, Ed. R.K. Dhawan, Delhi, Prestige Books, 1991, pp. 86-88.

Maya's love of life; she feels that she has a greater justification to live."[5]

In Maya's memory the image of Shiva invokes in her a *shloka* about Natraj :

> "The bronze Shiva, dancing just a shade outside the ring of lamp-light, ... fixed. And yet there was nothing bronze or immobile in this pose of eternal creative movement ... graceful foot upon the squirming body of evil, and the raised leg... raised into a symbol of liberation... the wise, remote face... my rag-picking memory had retained... and now suddenly bobbed upon this day that had dragged through near annihilation to supreme aliveness. 'Calling by the beat of the drum all persons engrossed in worldly affairs, the kind-hearted. One who destroys all fear of the meek and gives them reassurance, and points by his hand to his upraised lotus foot as the refuge of salvation and also carries the fire and who dances in the Universe, let that Lord of the Dance protect us...." "The sonorous Sanskrit syllables rang richly in my mind,..." (*CP*, pp. 203-204).

Another aspect of Natraj symbolism is that it is supreme aliveness. P.K. Pandeya finds it as Maya's vision, a sense of stillness and permanence :

> "In the Hindu psyche of Maya this vision and the memory of the *shloka*, about Shiva is pregnant and this gives her a sense of security, and as she says "supreme aliveness". In this constant flux, only art and God can give a sense of stillness, permanence and eternity. Here we have the bronze Shiva and the conceptual Shiva who protects the meek. As the peacock has religio-cultural suggestions so is this vision of Maya."[6]

Cry the Peacock is a poetic novel with dense imagery. Her descriptions are poetic. Maya is not only emotionally starved but sexually also. Her frustration is of not getting physical pleasure, she expresses her dissatisfaction in the following manner. It is an act of delicate violence shown on jasmine buds :

> "In a damp, white handkerchief, gathered into a nest, lay a heap of white jasmine buds that the gardener had plucked from the dawnfresh hedges that morning, for me to thread into garlands for my hair and wrists, and which, for some reason, I had forgotton. There they lay, almost palpitating with living breath, open, white, virginal. I plunged my face into them and kissed them with a wild longing to pierce

5. *Op. cit.*, p. 18.

6. P.K. Pandeya, *op. cit.*, p. 91.

through that unimpeachable immaculate chastity of whiteness, to the very soul of their maddening fragrance. What dreams they conjured in swirls of scent, what passions, what scenes of love and farewell... I tore myself away from them, having bruised them with my kisses, and trembling, flung them against the mirror, at that fleeting image to which they belonged, and backed out of the room which was now terrorised by the vast, purple shadows of a dreadful night'' (*CP*, pp. 106-107).

Maya's overcharged sensibilities are described through animal imagery, on one hand there is the magestic image of the peacock, and on the other the grotesque. This is how her neurotic state is described through a vision:

> ``Wild horse, white horse, galloping up paths of stone, flying away into the distance, the wild hills. The heights, the dizzying heights of my mountains, towering, tapering, edged with cliff-edges, founded on rock. Fall, fall, gloriously fall to the bed of racing rivers, foaming seas. Horrid arms, legs, tentacles thrashing, blood flowing, eyes glazing. Storm — storm at sea, at land! Fury. Whip. Lash, Fly furiously. Danger! Danger! The warning rings and echoes, from far, far, far. Run and hide, run and hide – if you can, miserable fool ! Ha, ha. Fool, fool.

And we are informed later that this vision is caused by fever:

> ``I am in a fever. Stop me! Silence me! Or I will fly on, fly up, at you, through you, past you, and away. For I am ill. I am in a fever, God, in a fever.''

Cry the Peacock uses technique of fantasy. Desai describes the inner loneliness of Maya and the vision described above tells of her mental state. It is creditable that in her first novel Anita Desai has given such inner probing of Maya's psyche. The novel has earned good comments as ``A poetry-novel, has a great sense of place'' *(Sunday Telegraph,* U.K.). Moon symbolism is also used in the novel. It is on a moon-lit night when Maya pushes Gautama off the roof. And the reason for immediate provocation was that Gautama came between her and ``the worshipped moon.

> ``And then we turned again, walking towards the terraced end now, and I saw, behind the line of trees that marked the horizon, the pale hushed glow of the rising moon. I held him there, while I gazed at it watching the rim of it climb swiftly above the trees, and then walked towards it in a dream of love. At the parapet edge, I paused, made him pause, and his words were lost to me as I saw the moon's vast, pure

> surface, touched only faintly with petals of shadow, as though brushed by a luna moth's wings, so that it appeared a great multifoliate rose, waxen white, virginal, chaste and absolute white, casting a light that was holy in its purity, a soft, suffusing glow of its chastity, casting its reflection upon the night with a vast, tender mother love.
>
> And then Gautama made a mistake — his last, decisive one. In talking, gesturing, he moved in front of me, thus coming between me and the worshipped moon, his figure an ugly, crooked grey shadow that transgressed its sorrowing chastity. 'Gautama!' I screamed in fury, and thrust out my arms towards him, out at him, into him and past him, saw him fall then, pass through an immensity of air, down to the very bottom'' (*CP*, p. 208).

Thus the novel is rich in technique using language in poetic manner and thus the novelist is able to explore and portray the psyche of Maya who after killing her husband goes back to her father's house at Lucknow and retrogress to her childhood days, lost in her toys and the happy world of the childhood.

The novel has been rightly described as a psychological novel. R.S. Sharma writes:

> ''*Cry the Peacock,* Anita Desai's first novel is also perhaps the first step in the direction of psychological fiction in Indian writing in English. Initially the novel shocks us with its neurotic and near morbid obsession with death, but on a closer study, we admire the writer's skill in capturing the psychic states of a woman haunted by an awareness of death.''[7]

Thus Anita Desai's novel *Cry the Peacock* is a technically well written novel.

Her second novel *Voices in the City* (1965) is an interesting novel and the title itself is an example of technique. Some critics have observed that in the novel the city is important, and is skilfully handled by her, they have compared it with that of Dicken's London and Hardy's Egdon-Heath. A.V. Krishna Rao thinks that the city of Calcutta, not Nirode is the hero of the novel:

> ''Thus although one may be tempted to consider Nirode as the hero of the Novel, the city of Calcutta is indeed the invisible protagonist of the novel. Calcutta, conceived as a force of creation, preservation

---

7. R.S. Sharma, *Anita Desai*, New Delhi, Arnold Heinemann, 1981, p. 24.

> and destruction is ultimately identified as a symbol for the goddess Kali."[8]

No one can deny the importance of the city in the novel. The blurb in the novel also mentions it :

> "Based on the life of the middle class intellectuals of Calcutta, it is an unforgettable story of a Bohemian brother and his two sisters caught in the cross-currents of changing social values. In many ways the story reflects a vivid picture of India's social transition — a phase in which the older elements are not altogether dead, and the emergent ones not fully evolved."

Another part of the blurb says, "The city grips the reader from the very first page... Calcutta evidently can be as Paris... a readable novel, without many false notes" (*Tribune*).

The city is described in much detail, an opressive city, a dying city but all the same exercising a powerful influence on all the three characters. This has been amply made clear in the Amla Section of the novel. The city has been described as a monster city :

> ".... That this monster city that lived no normal healthy, red-blooded life but one that was subterranean, underlit, stealthy and odorous of mortality, had captured and enchanted — or disenchanted both her sister and brother."[9]

The novel begins at Howrah Station where Nirode has come to see-off his brother Arun who is going to England for higher studies. Coming out of the station Nirode gives a powerful naturalistic description of Calcutta with all its squalor and apathy :

> ... the drain was choked with the sodden remnants of partings and farewells. Beating his way out of the swarming apathy of Howrah, Nirode strode down the bridge, dodging the traffic that made the bridge roar and rattle beneath his feet like a tunnel of bones and steel. Trams crashed murderously past him handcarts rolled recklessly, maniacally by. Nirode thrust them all away with arms that never moved, thrust all the thunder away, thinking his thoughts in such vivid, short-lived streaks of lightning as those that made the tramlines spark and quiver... dark pandemonium... (*VC*, p. 7) .

8. A.V. Krishna Rao, *Voices in the City, A Study : Perspectives on Anita Desai*, Ed. Ramesh K. Srivastava, Ghaziabad, Vimal Prakashan, 1984, p. 175.

9. Anita Desai, *Voices in the City*, Delhi, Orient Paperbacks, 1965, p. 150. All further references in the novel shall be incorporated in the body. Henceforth the novel is referred to in abbreviated form as *VC*.

Later in the novel there is another description of the city. This time it is from the pages in Monisha's diary. She finds living in Calcutta an ordeal and she thinks of Kalimpong. Very nicely she puts it, she finds the city without conscience :

> "There is no diving underground in so overpopulated a burrow, even the sewers and gutters are chocked, they are also full. Of what? Of grime, darkness, poverty, disease? Is that what I mean — or the mertriciousness, the rapacity, the uneasy lassitude of conscience? Has this city a conscience at all, this Calcutta that holds its head between its knees and grins toothlessly up at me from beneath a bottom black with the dirt that it sits on?... . There are no ethics in these houses of trade, any more than there is anything aesthetic in the little plaster idols. Ethics are shunned, all is shunned except the swelling and fattening of the iron safe and of mortal, male flesh.... I see another face of this devil city, a face that broods over the smouldering fire — a dull, vacant, hopeless face. The rickshaw, coolie, the street sweeper, the tanner, the beggar child with his limbs cut off at the joints, the refugee who litters the platforms of Sealdah Station with his excrement and offspring — they share one face, one expression of tiredness, such overwhelming tiredness that even bitterness is merely passive and hopelessness makes the hand extend only feebly, then drop back without disappointment. Two faces — one rapacious, one weary — gaze at me from every direction" (*VC*, pp. 116-118).

The picture is of confusion absolute hence the title *Voices in the City*. And more pertinent thing in the novel to observe is section division of the novel which is, "Nirode," "Monisha," "Amla" and "Mother." The city does have influence on Nirode, Monisha and Amla but it doesn't have much influence on the mother because she lives away, far from the madding crowd at Kalimpong.

Anita Desai also uses the technique of symbolism in the novel. The city itself is symbolic but there is also nature symbolism in section III 'Amla'. She has arrived recently in Calcutta to begin her professional career of commercial artist. She is exhausted and the decaying nature in Monisha's house garden very well externalises mental state of Amla. It is the ruin of once well maintained garden but now everything is chaotic with a depressing effect, even the statues have lost blood :

> "She sat down abruptly on the marble stairs that led to it — a flight of them, cracked and held together only by its lining of damp moss.

On two posts that flanked the steps stood blind, disspirited marble goddesses — the Greek idol copied and recopied till the last drop of immaculate blood had been sucked out of it — holding what looked like ugly metal cages for Birds of Paradise long flown from them. Actually they were meant to shelter lamps that lit the stairs on gala evenings, but Amla could not remember and nor, for that matter, could her aunt, when last such an evening had enlivened this dank, unbreathing garden where the unmown grass housed singing swarms of mosquitoes, and spider webs alone multiplied and reproduced amidst the leaves of plantains and mango trees that had years ago surrendered the desire to propagate and fructify. Only a few grotesquely crooked temple trees were starred with bridal flowers and, at the edges of the grass, a row of tuberoses closed thick white petals about their secret scent. The half-hearted lights of neighbouring houses looked down upon this pocket of decrepitude and darkness and were not bright enough to illumine it'' (*VC*, p. 148).

The above depressive description of the ill-kept garden shows negative aspects of nature. Nature instead of being life giving and refreshing is as though sucking the blood of human beings. The lifelessness of nature is subtly suggested by the imitation Greek statues which are so far removed from the Greek idol that as though the last drop of immaculate blood had been sucked out of them.

The nature imagery here externalises the mental state of Amla, as though she too has been sucked out of vitality. The thrill and excitement of reaching a big city has disappeared and there is nothing but despair and exhaustion.

> ``All the tingle and the thrill of entering the big city, of beginning a new career, all that now curled up inside her tired head and went to sleep. She was aware only of this giant exhaustion growing and swelling inside her, of a feeling of sick apprehension and despair'' (*VC*, p. 149).

The above instance illustrates well Anita Desai's fictional technique because externalising the ``inscape'' of a character is not easy because emotions are abstract things and for a creative writer externalising inner feelings is an artistic challenge. In order to do this one resorts to different kinds of literary techniques.

Nirode's complex parental relationship has been commented upon by various critics. His relationship with his mother is that of love and hate. She is both his ideal as well as object of repugnance. For him she is both the heroine and the vamp. Throughout the novel we come across this theme but in the context of the present chapter what is more important is just how deftly this complex relationship has been portrayed and to do so Anita Desai resorts to a subtle technique, that of describing through a dream of Nirode. This dram is not an escape into fantasy, nor it is, to use Freudian term, a wish-fulfilment dream. The description of the dream is not only an example of Anita Desai's technique's excellence but also of her mastery in psychological probing. She is not only good at portraying feminine psyche, as we have seen in chapter second of the book, but also at unbaring male psyche. As we know, in dream world no law of reality operates and therefore the dream as fictional technique is aptly used here. The dream not only brings back the past and his dead father but also presents the present worry of Nirode over his mother's suspected adulterous relationship with Major Chadha.

Nirode has no control over reality but certainly in dreams he may have some control even if dreams cannot be willed. In real life he can only hate his mother because of her suspected adultery, by not opening her letters, not asking money from her, not accepting any help from her and being apathetic towards her but in his dream he forbids her to carry on her affair with Major Chadha :

> "Anger and impotence tore at the light sheet of his sleep, tore holes into it that admitted a new, harsh and uncoloured light upon the dream scene. Something about all this prettiness and brightness turned macabre and horrifying, and he soon saw why : he himself was not an inhabitant of it, he stood some distance away from it, and between him and his mother's brilliant territory was erected a barbed wire fence, all glittering and vicious. To his astonishment, he found at his side, also on the wrong side of this cruel division, his father lying slovenly in the prickled shadow of the barbs, asleep, his mouth half-open, the buttons of his silk coat undone. He looked back at his mother to ask her to explain this unsightly apparition of the dead man, but she looked not at him but at his father, and in the curve of her mouth and the sullen lowering of her brows there was so much contempt and resentment that she seemed to forget herself in this passion. Then something distracted her, footsteps, a voice, and she turned to greet, with a ravishing smile,her neighbour, that retired Major, or Brigadier who, with his bestial jaws and small eyes and hairy hands repelled Nirode, made him shrink away, watching the large bumbling creature grope at the garden gate, walk past the clump of bamboo dahlias, then the pear tree, the row of azaleas, to

where his mother sat on the veranda, smiling a slow, sensual smile. Hideous to see in his mother, hideous to see in the heroine who had led his crusade. He turned over, away from her, and in his sleep groaned, for with Nirode sleep was no deeper than the thin sheet that covered him, and it was riddled with holes spanned by ineffectual darning.

Sonny awoke to hear him say, 'No, mother you can't,'..."

(*VC*, pp. 27-28).

In the above extract Anita Desai very well portrays the ambiguous feeling of Nirode towards his mother. In the novel we are informed that he had adored his mother since his childhood and even later when he is grown-up and apparently hates her,he is not free from his mother's charm and attraction. In the above instance we not only find good views of fictional technique but also how the technique becomes the vehicle of theme. Psychological portrayal, use of symbolism and dream are some of the important fictional technique that have been used by Anita Desai in *Voices in the City*.

Her third novel *Bye-Bye Black Bird* (1971) is a novel of a broader canvas. Not that it does not have psychological probing but it deals more with social reality in the life of Indian immigrants in England. The common fictional technique of contrasting characters can be seen in Dev and Adit. in the beginning Adit is Anglophile and his newly arrived Indian friend Dev from Calcutta is critical of everything English, despite being brought up on English literature and having known Britain right in India through :

"... the pages of Dickens and Lamb. Addison and Boswell, Dryden and Jerome; not in colour and in three dimensions as he now encountered them, but in black and white ... yet how exact the reproductions had been, how accurate, he realised as he recognised the originals, around him, within reach at last."[10]

But by the end of the novel the roles change, the English hater stays back in London, in this friend's shoes, being employed in his friend's place and living in his flat, and the Anglophile realising the hollowness of his life in London, pretending what he is not, leading a sham life he decides to leave England for good for his country, to his roots howsoever materially backward and monetarily poor. This is a good use of technique of

10. Anita Desai, *Bye-Bye Black Bird*, Delhi, Orient Paperbacks, 1985, p. 10. All further subsequent references to the novel shall be incorporated in the body. Henceforth the novel is referred to in abbreviated form as *BBBB*.

contrasting characters. Another use of this technique is to be found in Sarah's character and that of other Indian women who have totally adjusted to England. Another Anglicised character is Mr. Krishna Swami Krishnamurthy, B.A. (Cantab) who hates going back to India but does want to start fishing business in South India. Dev in his search for a job replies to an advertisement and speaks to Krishna Swami on telephone and the impression that he gets of him is that of a British man seeking to do business in India but he is totally wrong in his impression :

> "The smooth Oxbridge accents that had slid down the telephone wires earlier that morning had led him to expect someone sleek, pink and British, an adventurous city man seeking to extend his empire to the fabled India of silks and tiger skins. Instead, here was a young Indian of distinctly Dravidian complexion dressed ostentatiously..." (*BBBB,* p. 112).

Both Krishna Swami and Dev are contrasts to Adit.

Anita Desai also makes use of certain Hindi words in her dialouges but their use is justified. Justification for using foreign words is that either the words are untranslatable or the words that come spontaneously when the character is emotionally charged. The words belonging to the first category are *Papadums, Halwa, Char-chari, Pooja* and the like. The words belonging to the second category are *Hai hai, yar, paji, Arebaba, Namak Haram* and so on so forth. Anita Desai makes use of her rhetorical skill when Dev is haranguing. Dev believes that he is a cultural ambassador to England and wants to reverse the historical fact of colonisation of India by the British; he wants the reversal of it by colonisation of England by Indians. The whole speech is both comical and fantastic with a touch of wishfulness but at the same time it does sound absurd, for history cannot be reversed. The other aspect of this speech is that as during the British rule lots of Englishmen came to India similarly later so many Indians immigrated to England as to create their small India in London. The fact is that a locality called South Hall in London is dominated by Indians and being there one does not feel that one is thousands of miles away from India, with Indian shops, Indian restaurants and shops selling sarees and salvar suits, but back to Dev's harangue :

> "Let history turn the tables now. Let the Indian traders come to England — the Sikhs and Sindhis with their brass elephants and boxes of spice and tea. Let them take over the city, to begin with — let them move into Cheapside and Leadenhall and Cornhill. Let them move into Threadneedle Street and take over the Bank, the Royal Exchange and Guildhall. Then let them spread over the country —

the Sikhs with their turbans and swords and the Sindhis with their gold bars and bangles. Let them build their forts along the coast, in Brighton and Bristol and Bath. Then let our army come across, our Gurkhas and our Rajputs with the camel corps and elephants of Rajasthan''.... ''Let us abolish the British Railways! Down with Beeching down with Bradshaw! Let us set up our elephant routs and let the people travel in camel caravans. Let us bring across our yogis and gurus, barefoot and robed in saffron. Let us abolish the British public schools. Down with Eton, Harrow and all that bunkum! Let us replace Latin and Greek with the study of Sanskrit classics and Punjabi swear words. No one shall cook stews any more, or burghers and mash. Let us feed them all on chilli pickles, *tandoori* chicken and *rassum*. Let all British women take to the graceful saree and all British men to the noble *dhoti*...''

The above speech is a good example of demagougy in which although the meaning is not very sensible yet the force of language may very well be seen. It may be interpreted both as chauvinism and fantasy.

As in several other novels in this novel too Anita Desai makes use of poetry to convey the meaning more effectively. The title of the novel itself is aline from a poem and the poem is quoted more than once in the novel. On semantic level the line refers to Dev's farewell to immigrant Asians in England. Hence the word Black Bird. We are not sure whether the poem is in nursury rhyme or folk poetry or a poem composed by Anita Desai herself. What is more important is its thematic significance and how the poem is used at different places in the novel with different intentions. Its first occurrence is in chapter Ist where the poem is sung: ''Softly and sentimentally'' when he is strolling with Dev towards Highstreet:

> ''Pack up all my cares and woe,
> Here I go, singing low,
> Bye-Bye, Blackbird.
> Where somebody cares for me,
> Sugar is sweet and so is she,
> Bye-bye Blackbird'' (*BBBB*, p. 190).

The poem is quoted again in Chapter V but with different lines conveying different moods. The carefreeness and gaiety of the first instance is missing and instead here we find the mood of maladjustment and sorrow. In this instance the changed mood of Adit is obvious and so is his discomfiture in the alien country where people do not understand him.

This time he is singing softly :

> "Here no one can love or understand me,
> Oh what hard luck stories they all hand me.
> Make my bed and light the light,
> I'll arrive late tonight.
> Blackbird, bye-bye" (*BBBB*, p. 131).

The poem here suggests the gradual change coming here in Adit and his gradual disenchantment from his adopted country, his realisation of his phoney existence in England that would ultimately lead to his decision to leave England for good. The poem is quoted once again at the end of the novel where we realise its ultimate significance. As a matter of fact, the novel ends with these lines of the poem :

> "Make my bed and light the light,
> I'll arrive late tonight.
> Blackbird, bye-bye" (*BBBB*, p. 230).

Thus we find that the poem is organically woven in the tapestry of the novel. In other words it has structural significance. The poem describes different stages of Adit's character and also how his perception of England changes in the course of the novel.

Similarly a Vedic hymn to fire is quoted in Chapter III when Dev and Adit are travelling in a bus to Chelsea Bridge. When they pass through the Battersea powerstatic, Dev becomes the embodiment of Indian culture and he begins to "Intone, shrilly, in Sanskrit":

> "Produce thy streams of flames like a broad onslaught, Go forth impetuous like a king with his elephant. Thou are an archer. Send forth thy heat, thy winged flames..." (*BBBB*, p. 54).

In the present context quoting the Vedic hymn reflects Dev's anti-England stand and his desire to establish superiority of India over England which would later culminate in his harangue quoted earlier. This is not the only instance where Anita Desai quotes Sanskrit. We have already referred to the Sanskrit *shloka* about Natraj in *Cry the Peacock*. There are several other instances in *Bye-Bye Black Bird* where Anita Desai has used Folk poetry or Nursery rhymes in the novel, for instance, in the first Chapter we have three examples of which one is as follows :

> "Half a pound of tuppenny rice,
> Half a pound of treacle,
> Mix it up and make it nice..." (*BBBB*, p. 12).

In the same chapter we have other examples of Nursery rhymes such as:

"The north wind doth blow
And we shall have snow,
And what will poor Robin do then?" (*BBBB*, p. 21).

In Chapter II we come across another poem with the message to live life ungrudgingly. The poem is sung by Adit who is perfectly at home with *Agni* in England, whereas the fault finding, critical, almost cynical Dev is always worried. In this respect Adit is a foil to Dev for he lives "for the moments. I don't think. I don't worry." And he starts singing :

"For every evil under the sun
There is a remedy or there is none.
If there is one, seek till you find it,
If there is none, never you mind it" (*BBBB*, p. 49).

There are several other instances in the novel where poetry both literary (for example a poem by Wordsworth) and folk is used and such uses are strikingly relevant to theme and situation. In Chapter III Adit sings a song that expressed his released mental attitude in total contrast to Dev's complaining, never-at-ease mental state. In this instance once again Adit is singing a folk song :

"When I was a bachelor I lived by myself,

And all the bread and cheese I got, I laid upon the shelf.

The rats and the mice, they made such a strife,

I had to go to London to buy me a wife" (*BBBB*, p. 67).

Anita Desai also uses a German song with which IV Chapter ends and this shows her German Lineage. Since she does not give English paraphrase of the song we are not sure of the meaning yet from the context we can make out that it is a song of happiness. However, keeping in mind Adit's background from textual evidence his bursting out in a German song sounds unnatural for we are never told that he knows German or he has a German background.

Besides the use of poetry another technique that Anita Desai used in the novel is to quote certain slogans in the early part of the novel to give us a feel of London. It is a subtle device to make the reader feel that he is in London. Instead of using Cockney dialect she uses these sub-headings or slogans to give us the feel of London milieu. They are *Happiness is egg shaped. Guiness is good for you. You get there faster by train, Drinka Pinta, Milka day, keep, Britain Clean, Go To Work On An Egg.*

Even though as stated earlier *Bye-Bye Black Bird* is not as much concerned with psychological probings as Anita Desai's other novels, say for example, *Cry the Peacock* or *Fire on the Mountain,* yet we do have instances of Anita Desai's mastery in this area. At the end of Chapter II she very well describes the confused mental state of Sarah, her split-personality, her inability to comprehend Indian ethos for she belongs to a different culture. The following extracts describe well her confusion and the hypnogogic state of mind perfectly suggesting her perplexed mental state and her maladjustment with her husband and his culture in spite of her best efforts and willingness to understand, accept, and assimilate it :

> "After clearing the table, she went straight to bed with Kipling's plain tales from the hills and fell half-asleep listening to the rumble of talk and laughter in the next room, followed by the profuse strumming of sitars and pounding of drums on the spinning records. The music sounded all dissonance to her ears as did the voices, and she fell asleep from the fatigue of trying to place them, string them, compose them, into a pattern, a harmony. To her closed eyes the darkness moved in a tumult ofblack shapes that would not settle. Her dreams too were in pieces, tormented, like the night, slit and torn by long blades of rain" (*BBBB*, p. 50).

The novel is divided into three parts. The first part has no heading but the second and third are entitled "Discovery and Recognition," "Departure" respectively. This division is related to the thematic content of the novel. And this is yet another fictional technique used by Anita Desai to express her theme more systematically and effectively. As stated in the epigraph anything that contributes to telling the stories is a part of technique and from this point of view as compared with simple numerical chapter division this arrangement is more significant. Thus we find that *Bye-Bye Black Bird* which is considered not to be an important novel of Anita Desai does have instances of her fictional technique. Frankly speaking, her technique has not received adequate critical attention. The critics have been more preoccupied with her themes and other aspects of her novels.

Anita Desai's next novel is *Where Shall We Go This Summer* (1975). It is divided into three parts namely "Monsoon ('67)", "Winter ('47)" and "Monsoon' ('67)". The section division refers to the present and the past of the novel and thereby the childhood and the youth of the heroine Sita. The structure of the novel has received critical attention, and one of the critics finds the novel "strikingly familiar to that of Virginia Woolf's *The Light House.*"

It is observed that the structure of the novel is co-related with the content of the story :

> "The triptych structure of the novel neatly forms the pattern of the thesis, anti-thesis, and synthesis. Sita's consciousness develops through the process of consideration, rejection and then acceptance of the terms of life within this structure. She makes a new life for herself and is eager to let the new life in her to be borne in this world. It is said that she has to give up her individuality to some extent in order to accept; but only in this gesture is sanity."[11]

This structure also refers to the world of reality, the world of fantasy and the world of reality, again. As discussed earlier in Chapter III the novel deals with psychological probing of the mind of the heroine Sita who is pregnant but does not want to deliver the baby and insted goes to the Island of Manori where she has spent her childhood, thinking that the magical island would somehow stop the biological process of delivery. Thus Bombay represents the world of reality and Manori Island world of fantasy and Sita's return to reality. The city-Island dichotomy is so obviously symbolic that it has received critical attention, for example T.S. Anand observes:

> "Her desire to bear the child and return with Raman to the land signifies her return to life, community and society in spite of the debased dullness of life, the calamity, the lies and moral buggery, the odium, the detritus of wrong and sorrow dropped on every heart, for existence is not possible in an insulated stage of being, rather existence implies being with others."[12]

Since Sita had passed her carefree childhood on the island under the shadow of her legendary father she thinks that once she reaches the island every problem would be solved. The island for her was like prospero's enchanted island in *The Tempest.* She is so much under control of her childhood memories that even after being grown-up and having borne many children she is not able to free herself from the spell of the magic Island:

> "She had come here in order not to give birth.... Yet she had arrived, she was on the island, in order to achieve the miracle of not giving

---

11. Vimla Rao, "Where Shall We Go This Summer, An Analytical Study," *Indian Women Novelist*, Set I— III, ed. R.K. Dhawan, New Delhi, Prestige Books, 1991, pp. 176-177.

12. "Where Shall We Go This Summer? Anita Desai's stance against Negativism," *The Fiction of Anita Desai,* ed. R.K. Dhawan, New Delhi, Bahri Publications, 1989, p. 100.

birth. Wasn't this Manori, the island of miracles? Her father had made it an island of magic once, worked miracles of a kind. His legend was still here in this house — in the green tinge of the night shadows, the sudden slam of a wooden shutter, the crepitation of rain on the roof— and he might work another miracle, posthumously. She had come on a pilgrimage, to beg for the miracle of keeping her baby unborn.''[13]

This is her impression about the island in the 1st section of the novel when she is a grown-up woman. Since her childhood and adolscence was spent on the island with a limited exposure hence even though physically grown-up she had a mind of a child and she regarded the island as the magic island where miracles were possible.

> ''She was not really a child at that time in another environment she might have already been regarded as a young woman but she had lived a strange life, an unusual life, that had the effect of making her withdraw into the protective chrysalis of childhood for longer than is usual for most. She saw the island as a piece of magic, a magic mirror — it was so bright, so brilliant to her eyes after the tensions and shadows of her childhood. It took her some time to notice that this magic, too cast shadows'' (*WSWGS*, p. 63).

Sita's habit of smoking is also symbolic of her desire not to give birth to the baby. Although in the beginning she smokes to spite her in-laws yet later when she becomes pregnant the habit could be injurious to the foetus. K.P. Ambekar has observed the use of bird symbolism in the novel. Sita sees herself as a wounded eagle :

> ''Like Maya in *Cry the Peacock*, for whom the dance of Peacock is the symbol of love and death [''Living they (Peacocks) are aware of death, dying they are in love with life''], Sita sees herself as a wounded eagle. The crows represent the callous society around her. In the first incident of the novel, Sita finds that crows are joyously screeching and pecking at something on the ledge below the balcony of her flat. It is an eagle, injured and unable to fly. She is infuriated at the crows and tries to drive them away with the help of a toy gun. But Sita knows that the wounded eagle has really no chance of survival against the attack of crows, though she does not admit it openly.''[14]

---

13. Anita Desai, *Where Shall We Go This Summer*, Delhi, Orient Paperbacks, 1982, p. 31. All subsequent references to the novel shall be incorporated in the body.

14. K.P. Ambekar, ''Symbolism in Where Shall We Go This Summer?'' *Indian Women Novelist* III, *op. cit.*, p. 203.

Another important technique that she uses in the novel is use of poetry but unlike in *Bye-Bye Black Bird* here the poems quoted are more serious. She quotes her favourite Greek poet C. P. Cavafy's. The poem quoted reflects her own philosophy and the kind of characters she likes to create. The poem occurs in the last section of the novel and it comes as a revelation to Sita. If her husband Raman had the courage to face the realities of life and discharge his duties then "She reminded herself that she had courage, too, the courage of being a coward." And here is that the second part of the poem quoted :

> "*He who refuses does not repent. Should he be asked again, he would say No again. And yet that No — the straight No — crushed him for the rest of his life*" (*WSWGS*, p. 139).

Her husband Raman is a totally different kind of character who believes "Life must be continued, and all its business" and that is why his children looked up to him and respected him and for a man like him are quoted these lines of the Cavafy poem :

> "*To certain people there comes a day*
> *When they must say the great Yes or the great No.*
> *He who has the Yes ready within him*
> *reveals himself at once, and saying it crosses over*
> *to the path of honour and his own conviction*" (*WSWGS*, p. 139).

The quoted poem is an expression of Anita Desai's own conviction about the kind of characters she likes to create. In one of her interviews she accepts :

> "I am interested in characters who are not average but have retreated, or have been driven into some extremity of despair and to turn against, or made a stand against the general current. It is easy to flow with the current it makes no demands, it costs no effort, but those who cannot follow it, whose heart cries out 'the great No' who fight the current and struggle against it, they know what the demands are and what it costs to meet them."[15]

There is one more example of use of the poetry in the novel and this time it is a poem by D.H. Lawrence and this too occurs in the last part of the novel. Sita had been trying to recollect these lines but she had failed. And finally she recollects them and the lines come to her as a revelation. And these lines are:

> "*The wild young heifer, glancing distraught,*
> *With a strange, new knocking of life at her side*

15. "Yashodhar Dalmia's Interview with Anita Desai," *The Times of India*, April 29, 1979.

Runs seeking a loneliness.
The little grain draws the earth, to hide,
Nay, even the slumbrous egg as it labours under the shell
Patiently to divide and sub-divide,
Asks to be hidden, and wishes nothing to tell'' (*WSWGS*, p. 150).

Anita Desai herself has commented upon the significance of these lines in the novel in one of her interviews suggesting that one has to make compromises to live in this world :

> ''Of course, if one is alive in this world one cannot survive without compromise, drawing the line means certain death and in the end, Sita opts for life with compromise — consoling herself with Lawrence's verse with the thought that she is compelled to make this tragic choice because she is a part of the earth, of life, and can no more reject it than the slumbrous egg can or the heifer or the grain.''[16]

Thus Lawrence's poem provides vision to Sita to live life, to accept reality, to go back to Bombay and deliver the baby. What Raman's persuasions could not do what rational argument could not do is done by the poem.

Such is the power of poetry and that is why Anita Desai uses poetry in her novels as a fictional technique. This is not the only novel where she uses this technique as we have seen earlier and would find in her later novels too.

Her next novel *Fire on the Mountain* (1977) is a novel in which she makes use of symbolism. She also makes use of the flash back technique in narrating the story. The novel centres around the character of Nanda Kaul, the widow of vice-chancellor who is compelled both by choice and circumstances to live in seclusion in an old bunglow in Kasauli. The novel also makes use of fantasy and it is Nanda Kaul who lives in the world of fantasy. In order to engage attention of her grand-daughter Raka she spins several fantastic tales about her father. It is interesting to note that it is a grown-up person and not the child who goes into the world of fantasy. The use of fantasy in the novel has attracted critical attention and one of the critics has observed that Anita Desai has used fantasy not only in this novel but in her other novels too. This is how she has described the use of fantasy and various purposes for which it is used in the novel :

16. Atma Ram, ''An Interview with Anita Desai,'' *World Literature Written in English*, XVI (1), November 1977, pp. 95-104.

"... Self revelation is not the main thrust of fantasy in *Fire on the Mountain* which uses it in an entirely different way. It is not bordering on hallucination. Two kinds of fantasy would exist side by side; one which is consciously and deliberately woven by Nanda Kaul to interest her great grand-daughter Raka, the other which is shared by Raka and Ram Lal and is based on his belief in the supernatural... Raka's private world of Fantasy is somewhere between the two — it is neither wholly and naturally accepted fact as the *Churails* are for Ram Lal, nor is it a lie woven for self-preservation — In *Fire on the Mountain,* fantasy also exists purely at the level of imagery as a part of the self analysis which some of the characters carry on."[17]

In the very first chapter nature imagery has been used to portray the character of Nanda Kaul. She has had such a busy family life that in the evening of her life she wants to do nothing with family or society. She prefers her lonely isolated existence guarding her privacy fiercely and the news of Raka's arrival, conveyed to her through a letter, unsettles her. What she wanted was total withdrawal from society and hating human society so much so as to yearn to be a tree, a part of nature. In the authorial description in the Chapter I a parallel has been shown between her and a tree:

"She was grey, tall and thin and her silk saree made a sweeping, shivering sound and she fancied she could merge with the pine trees and be mistaken for one. To be a tree, no more and no less, was all she was prepared to undertake" (*FOM,* p. 1).

But human beings cannot be trees howsoever they may yearn for it. This is the only novel of Anita Desai in which nature plays such a vital role on the level of symbolism and imagery and it has to be accepted that she makes effective use of this technique to portray different characters. The title itself deals with nature. The Fire and the Mountain both are natural phenomena. However, in this instance the fire is man-made, to be more specific Raka made. Although at times forest is a fire on its own a happening called in Sanskrit दावाग्नि (Forest conflagration), why does Raka set the mountain on fire is a different question which does not come in the scope of the present chapter.

We also come across the use of nature symbolism and imagery of wild nature in the context of Raka's character who is emotionally deprived and

17. Jasbir Jain, *Stairs to the Attic : The Novels of Anita Desai,* Jaipur, Printwell Publishers, 1987, pp. 47-51.

comes from a broken home. She is an unnatural child not interested in the fantastic tales of Nanda Kaul and she usually keeps her to herself. She is attracted towards the unpleasant aspects of nature like, the barren spaces of the valley. This attraction is an externalisation of her sub-normal nature. The cosy-civilised world does not attract her, rather it is the uncompromising and lawless nature that pulls her :

> "This hill, with its one destroyed house and one unbuilt one, on the ridge under the fire-singed pines, appealed to Raka with the strength of a strong sea-current — pulling, dragging. There was something about it — illegitimate, uncompromising and lawless — that made her tingle. The scene of devastation and failure somehow drew her, inspired her... . It was the ravaged, destroyed and barren spaces in Kasauli that drew her : the ravine where yellow snakes slept under grey rocks and agaves growing out of the dust and rubble, the skeletal pines that rattled in the wind, the wind-levelled hill-tops and the seared remains of the safe, cosy, civilised world in which Raka had no part and to which she owed no attachment" (*FOM*, pp. 90-91).

Here nature imagery is a device to portray the character of Raka. Since she is deprived of parental love, she finds no interest in family or society. She finds more solace and interest in nature and that too in her wilder mood. Like the untamed lawless nature she too is stubborn and does not bother about her *Nani*. All the efforts on Nanda Kaul's part fail to interest her. The parallel between the untamed nature and her abnormal behaviour which culminates in her setting the mountain on fire is made clear when one day after her usual ramblings in the forest she comes back to "carignano," the bunglow where Nanda Kaul lives, chanting under her breath definitely and inaudibly, "I don't care — I don't care — I don't care for anything." The barren nature that attracts her is suggestive of emotionally barren family background from which she comes.

As in other novels in *Fire on the Mountain* too Anita Desai uses poetry and this time it is a poem by G.M. Hopkins. Although here the use of poem is not so significant yet it has some connection with the character of Nanda Kaul who quotes it and the poem signifies her desire to be away from humdrum of life, to a heaven of nature far from the madding crowd.

After quoting the poem it is explained that the poem is not about a geographical location but it is about a Nur's vocation, "but, all the same, it seemed to apply." And this is the poem :

> "I have desired to go
> Where springs not fail,

To fields where flies no sharp and sided hail
And a few lilies blow.
And I have asked to be
Where no storms come,
Where the green swell is in the havens dumb,
And out of the swing of the sea'' (*FOM*, p. 58).

There are some other poems quoted in the novel but they are not so significant. We would like to say that in this novel the use of poetry does not carry a vision as in *Where Shall We Go This Summer*? Nevertheless, the use of poetry is a fictional device that Anita Desai uses in the novel to communicate her meaning more effectively.

Anita Desai's seventh novel *In Custody* (1984) is the story about a teacher (Deven) who is to interview an Urdu poet living in Old Delhi. Deven is so fascinated by the personality of the poet Nur that he is never able to come out of his shadow. From the point of view of technique the first thing to be noticed is the title. There are two implications of the title. The first as warranted by the text that Deven is the true disciple of Nur and he would keep his poetry in safe custody. Deven is superior to the flattering crowd that sorrounds Nur :

> ''This was the audience Nur had always had to try his verses on, Deven saw, revolted by their flattery, and he knelt behind Nur in reverential silence, watching him write, keeping himself apart from the others, the one true disciple in whose safe custody Nur could place his work.''[18]

But the other implication of the title is one complication after the other in which Deven lands himself. He has to take great pains in order to interview the poet. And finally when the interview does take place it is a fiasco, for the tape-recorder has not been operated properly. But Nur and his wife pester Deven for money since they have been instrumental in materialising the interview and so it seems that Deven's life is in custody of Nur and his family. Even up to the end of the novel the letter keeps coming from Nur asking Deven for money for his son, for his treatment and for going to *Haj* as though Deven is responsible for everything. Deven's mind is so taxed as if he would break down. By the end of the novel he has a disturbing vision, a negative vision. It is not the vision which would illumine him to face life, as in the case of Sita in *Where Shall We Go This Summer?* or Bim in *Clear Light of Day*. It is a nightmarish

18. Anita Desai, *In Custody*, London, William Heinemann Limited, 1984, p. 168. All further references to the novel shall be incorporated in the body. Henceforth the novel is referred to in abbreviated form as *IC*.

vision in which Deven finds himself hopelessely trapped. This vision may be compared with the neurotic vision of Maya in *Cry the Peacock* although Deven is no neurotic. In the last page of the novel Deven is wondering where is the end or if there is any end and then he has a vision :

> "He had a vision of Nur's bier, white, heaped with flowers, rose and marigold, bright blazing flowers on the white sheet. He saw the women in the family weeping and wailing around it. He heard the funeral music play. He saw the shroud, the grave — open. When Nur was laid in it, would this connection break, this relation end? No, never — the bills would come to him, he would have to pay for the funeral, support the widows, raise his son..." (*IC*, pp. 203-204).

Thus the title of the novel is very significant but curiously enough no critic has addressed himself to this vital aspect of the novel which is a part of Desai's fictional technique. However, at least one critic has written about the use of fantasy in narrative technique of the novel, observing :

> "It develops the theme of adventure, the attraction of the unusual... fantasy lies here in the narrative technique which combines the realistic and the romantic modes. It is not character which is important but incident or situation."[19]

As in her other novels in *In Custody* also there are references to poetry. This time the poems are recited by Nur himself but significantly Nur's own poetry is never quoted, rather it is Nur's favourite English poets who are quoted. And the quoted poets are the famous romantics like Byron, Shelley and Keats and the lines quoted are from *Ode to the Westwind, Ode to a Nightingale* and *La Belle Dame Sans Merci*. The poems quoted have some bearing upon Nur's character as inferred by Deven :

> "The recitation was so long, so filled with finely timed pauses and gestures, that Deven had begun to wonder if it did not have some bearing upon that aspect of the poet's private life into which he had unwillingly had such a terrifying glimpse, and had even begun to see certain psychological connections..." (*IC*, p. 157).

The plot of the novel is intricately connected with the characters of Deven and Nur. In the beginning it is Deven through whose action the plot moves but as soon as Murad asks him to interview the poet the actions are more controlled by the poet rather than by Deven or Murad. The central incident of the novel is the interview and all other actions are related to and subordinate to it. It is true that the main doer is Deven but all his

19. *Stairs to the Attic, op. cit.*, p. 53.

actions, his long effort and several trips to Delhi to interview the poet are subject to the wills of Nur. The action of the whole novel is a long series of episodes related to the interview. And at long last when the interview does take place it does not come out well. The tone of the novel is ironical in the sense that in spite of the best efforts of Deven, circumstances go against him and everything leads him to trouble – Jan sells him a second hand tape-recorder and the boy Chiku who has to operate the tape-recorder operates it on wrong time and what is finally recorded is worthless, babblings of Nur about biryani, pigeon flights, wrestling bouts of his youth interpersed with abuses. Thus from the point of view of technique it is not a very significant novel, but still it very well portrays the mind of an anti hero, Deven who is different, unsure of himself, never able to fight and always a victim of people and circumstances.

Anita Desai's fifth novel *Clear Light of Day* (1980) is once again a family drama covering a long period of time beginning from childhood of the Das children to their maturity and historically two periods that of colonial and independent India. The novel has elicited criticism but little on the technique aspect. Jasbir Jain comments on the use of fantasy in the novel.[20] Seema Jena writes "the plot succeeds in featuring the vision of the author which explains that love, understanding and forgiveness are qualities which triumph over despair and destruction."[21] S.R. Jamkhandi focuses attention on the central image of the home of Bim and traces the relationships of different characters in the house.[22]

Anita Desai makes use of poetry in the novel but what is more important is that she quotes lines from two poems by Emily Dickinson and T.S. Eliot as epigraphs to the novel. The first epigraph has the following lines of Emily Dickinson:

> Memory is a strange bell —
> Jubilee and Knell

The significance of these two lines is that memories of the past play an important role in the novel and they are juxtaposed with the present as mentioned in the blurbs "Memories of the past coalesce with the tensions and jealousies of the present in this sharply drawn and sorrowful portrait of the ebb and flow of sisterly love." In the context of Baba's character

---

20. J. Jain, *Stairs to the Attic, op. cit.*, p. 51.

21. *Voice and Vision of Anita Desai*, New Delhi, Ashish Publishing House, 1989, p. 75.

22. "Old Delhi revisited: Anita Desai's *Clear Light of Day*", *Commonwealth Fiction*, I, ed. R.K. Dhawan, New Delhi, Classical Publishing Co., 1987, pp. 245-252.

who is mentally retarded, memory plays even a very important role, because in his mind there are certain impressions that keep recurring. Because of his limited mental impressions he cannot go beyond them. He reminds us of the idiot character of Banjy in another powerful novel of family drama' *The Sound and the Fury* by William Faulkner.

The second epigraph is by T.S. Eliot describing the passage of time and how in spite time passing things don't change really, only the pattern changes:

See, now they vanish,
The faces and places, with the self which, as it
Could, loved them,
To become renewed, transfigured, in another pattern.

Not only Anita Desai herself has said that time plays an important role in the novel but at the end of the novel there is a quotation from T.S. Eliot's *Four Quartets*.

"Time the destroyer is time the preserver" which more or less reinforces the idea suggested in Eliot's quotation in the epigraph. This much about textual evidence and let us see what Desai herself says about the novel. She speaks about *Clear Light of Day* at two places but basically what she says is the same. In her interview in 1980 when the novel was published she had said:

> "My novel is set in Old Delhi and records the tremendous changes that a Hindu family goes through since 1947. Basically my preoccupation was with recording the passage of time: I was trying to write a four dimensional piece on how a family's life moves backwards and forwards in a period of time. My novel is about time as a destroyer, as preserver and about what the bondage of time does to people. I have tried to tunnel under the mundane surface of domesticity."[23]

Almost the same idea is repeated later when she says :

> What I have tried to prove is that although time appears to damage, destroy and extinguish one finds instead that nothing is lost, nothing comes to an end, but the spiral of life leads as much upwards as downwards and is in perpetual circular motion, both the past and the future existing always in time present."[24]

---

23. "Anita Desai, Tremendous Changes, Interview with Sunil Sethi," *India Today*, December 1-15, 1980, p. 142.

24. *Perspective on Anita Desai*, ed. R.K. Srivastava, Ghaziabad, Vimal Prakashan, 1984, pp. 224-225.

At least one critic of Anita Desai has taken note of her extensive use of poetry and other literary works used by her in the novel. Since one of the characters in the novel *Raja* is himself a poet therefore it is but natural that there should be a discussion of and reference to poetry. Santosh Gupta observes that the Das children, Raja, Bim, and Tara "Look beyond the house and try to know the world through books and literature as they do not have many opportunities of direct contact with the world."[25] There are quotations from English and Urdu poetry and such diverse poets as Tennyson, Byron, Swinburne, D.H. Lawrence, Eliot and Iqbal have been quoted. But the most important poet quoted is Iqbal, Raja's quoting of Iqbal shows his intense interest in Urdu poetry and although he quotes some very significant lines emphasising the importance of man almost rubbing shoulders with God, but it is hardly possible for a young boy to fully realise the significance and meaning of the following lines :

> "Thou didn't create night but I made the lamp.
> Thou didn't create day but I made the cup
> thou didn't create the desert, mountains, and forests,
> I produce the orchards, gardens, groves. It is I who made the glass out of stone and it is I who turned a poison into an antidote" (50).

Raja may not understand the full significance of these lines but they do in corporate individualistic philosophy of Anita Desai. However, the most significant quotation from Iqbal comes at the end of the novel which is the vision of the novel similar to Lawrence's poem used in *Where Shall We Go This Summer*?

Santosh Gupta[26] happily comments:

> "In *Clear Light of Day*, also, Anita Desai, uses music and responses to it as a test of the protagonists sensitivity and maturity. It is also a reflection of the person's ability to experience emotions... . Music becomes symbolic of the intuitive understanding of oneself and of the reality that lies submerged under appearances."

But what are the words set to music that have such profound effect on Bim who is a teacher of history reading Gibbon's *Decline and Fall of Roman Empire*. There are words that provide vision to her and show the most significant use of poetry in the novel and they also throw light on the title of the novel. Now the words:

---

25. "Bringing the Portraits of Imagination and reason in *Clear Light of Day,*" Indian Women Novelists, *op. cit.*, p. 237.

26. Santosh Gupta, *op. cit.*, pp. 247-48.

"Your world is the world of fish and fowl. My world is the cry at dawn."

x x x

"In your world I am subjected and constrained, but over my world You have domination" (*CD*, pp. 182-183).

Certainly the poem has a spiritual note and goes beyond the mundane affairs of life but its significance lies in the fact that in order to live life with all its frustrations, disappointments, unfaithfulness and treachery to go beyond these mundane pettiness and to have a glimpse of the divine *i.e.* the *Clear Light of Day*. Usually Anita Desai's titles are significant as we have seen in case of *In Custody*. Similarly here also *Clear Light of Day* refers to Bim's revelation that removes clouds of grudge, dissatisfaction, and depression because of the treacherous behaviour of Raja who does not reciprocate Bim's feelings who sacrifices her life for the sake of the family. There is an authorial comment on the title of the novel which has a broad sympathetic attitude of forgiveness bringing to our minds the final mood of Shakespeare's romances.

The comment focuses on Bim and her retrospection :

"... Bim could see as well as by the Clear Light of Day that she felt only love and yearning for them all, and if there were hurts, these gashes and wounds in her side that bled, then it was only because her love was imperfect and did not encompass them thoroughly enough, and because it had flaws and inadequacies and did not extend to all equally. She didn't feel enough for her dead parents, her understanding of them was incomplete and she would have to work and labour to acquire it."

From the point of view of techniques the most important thing about this novel is the effective use of poetry. She also makes use of flashback technique which is appropriate, since the novel covers a long period of time, a generation as observed earlier.

Anita Desai's latest novel *Baumgartner's Bombay* (1988) is a novel that deals with the modern phenomenon of displaced persons. Like *Clear Light of Day*, this novel also covers a long period of time of almost fifty years beginning with the rise of Nazism in Germany to the late 1960s and 1970s. The locale of the novel are Germany and India. As in *Clear Light of Day* this novel too has an epigraph which is once again from T.S. Eliot. And this time from "East Coker" from *Four Quartrets* :

> "In my beginning is my end. In succession Houses rise and fall, crumble, are extended, are removed, destroyed, restored..."

In the context of the novel what signifies is the first line *i.e.* "In my beginning is my end," in the sense that Baumgartner's life, except for his short happy childhood is full of frustrations and misery. Since after leaving Germany he has neither a family nor familial relationship therefore "Houses rise and fall," has no significance for him except in his memories. Significantly in the very first chapter Baumgartner thinks of his mother and her endearing words for him, *'Meine Kleine Maus,' 'Mein Haschen', 'Liebchen...'* (*BB*, p. 3). He has preserved on the letters and postcards that he had received from his mother after he had left his fatherland in Germany for good. The first chapter of the novel uses flashback technique from the present to past and what a difference between the two the past prosperous and cosy and the present almost a tramp somehow making the two ends meet. His childhood is recalled through many of German songs and poems which are scattered throughout the novel. Unfortunately, since no English paraphrase to German is given, we cannot make out the meaning. Yet we can make out that some poems are songs to his happy childhood and later in the novel when he is a POW in British India there are songs describing Nazi Germany. Fortunately, in chapter four there is an English rendering of Nazi song which, however, has the significance for Baumgartner; because his race has been persecuted by the Nazis but he is compelled to participate along with other Germans. It is a song celebrating the fatherland along with description of the Rhine. The novel is full of German songs even though Baumgartner had forgotten his own mother tongue having been away from Germany for such a long time.

From the point of view of technique the novel is not very important except for the use of language. When Baumgartner arrives in Bombay he comes across a queer variety of English. He fails to comprehend what kind of language he is hearing. He had come to Bombay in order to begin a new life but coming to a new country with a different culture, people, and climate, he is bewildered. Anita Desai uses her skill in transcribing Indian pronunciation of English 'Ex-pawt. *Ofcourse*, ex-pawt. Germany, Europe, shipping, timber — I know, I know' (*BB*, p. 86). On his way from Bombay to Calcutta in the train there were two British soldiers in the compartment and although they were British, their English was foreign to him: "Yet Baumgartner could not understand a word, was not certain even that it was English. They rolled their words in their mouths, like potatoes. They were as foreign as those children on the platform – black, naked, raucous'' (*BB*, p. 90).

When in Calcutta he comes across another variety of English spoken by the prostitutes standing on the street. Anita Desai also transcribes their variety of English.

''Hoo-hoo, To-mmy,.... Less have drink, Tommy, come *awn.*'' (92)

Similarly another variety of English as spoken by British soldiers is to be found when Baumgartner tries to convince British Officer that he is not a Nazi German but a refugee in India but the officer would not listen to him:

> ''Stop that whining and show me your passport, will you? That's all yer asked for — yer passport, hear?''.... ''What Om I to do them.... ''Got a German passport, says you are born there — then what am I supposed to take you for, are bloomin' Indian?'' (*BB*, pp. 104, 106).

Such transciptions of English gives a realistic touch to Desai's portrayal of different kinds of characters in the novel. And this is a part of her fictional technique.

We also have example of Anita Desai's effective prose in describing an erotic scene without being too obvious touching the border of vulgarity yet suggesting everything that is needed. And the occasion is the copulation between Baumgartner and Lotte. Baumgartner is not very much interested in the act but it is forced upon him by the middle aged drunken Lotte. From the point of view of technique what is noteworthy is suggestiveness. For portraying eroticism in literature it is not necessary to go into gruesome details, as to be found in the novels of Shobha Dey, for example in *Starry Nights* and herein lies the mastery of Anita Desai. And this is how she describes the deed that has been eternal and is the cause of perpetuation of mankind on this earth:

> ''Like a cat she pressed upon him, nuzzling, nibbling, without speech. With small groans they made themselves comfortable against each other, finding concavities into which to press their convexities, and convexities into which to fit concavities, till at last they made one comfortable whole, two halves of a large misshapen bag of flesh, and then they were still and slept the heavy noontime sleep of the tropics, sighing and snoring less and less till they became totally immobile, silent'' (*BB*, p. 82).

The title of the novel is too straightforward to require any elucidation from the point of view of characterisation. Anita Desai has done justice to portray the mind of Baumgartner, his confusion, his maladjustment both in his own country and his adopted country and above all the pathos of his life, how he wanted to be accepted, but was never accepted whether in Germany or in India.

The above survey of fictional technique of Anita Desai found in her different novels shows that she uses different fictional techniques according to the demands of the story. Except for her use of poetry in her novels we may not call her a technical innovator, and who can be an innovator when the novel is being written in English for last two hundred years. From the point of view of technique what is important is not innovation or novelty but how effective the technique is in conveying the meaning and narrating the story effectively. We have novelists who use complicated fictional technique like the American novelists John Burroughs, but in the context of Anita Desai we have no hesitation to say that she is able to narrate the story, to portray the characters, to convey the mood, to evoke the atmosphere, to probe the psyche of her characters successfully. And for this she uses flashback technique, stream of consciousness technique, use of contrasting characters, use of symbolism and effective use of language either to evoke an atmosphere or to transcribe the pronunciations of characters or to use rhetorical skill for harangue. And to create realistic effect she also uses Hindi words but in moderation. The only thing that irks us is her use of German songs and poetry in her novels without giving English paraphrase, as though English readers whether in India or abroad are supposed to know German.

Chapter VI

CONCLUSION

The foregoing study of the theme and technique in the novels of Anita Desai leads us to draw certain inferences. The aspects of theme and technique in Anita Desai's novels are not isolated elements. They are inter-related at many levels of structure and texture. In order to convey her theme, the novelist judiciously uses character, situation, dialogues, and other elements in relation to the plot. The theme serves as the skeleton incorporating the whole life-perspective of the novelist through situations and scenes that are peculiar to her alone.

Cry the Peacock is a novel the theme of which may be described as an incompatible marriage with the focus on the heroine's psyche. Since she is a childless woman married to an unsympathetic, rational, down-to-earth man, it is but natural that she is lost in her own world, seeking solace in her childhood memories and recollecting her secured, cosy and pampered childhood. Since primarily it is a psychological novel, probling the workings of Maya's psyche, the narrative is not chronologically straight. There is a constant to and fro movement between the past and the present in the mind of Maya. The novel begins with the death of her pet dog Toto but thereafter the reader is taken from the present of the novel to the past of the heroine's life. Because of her lonely existence, childlessness, emotional deprivation, and want of reciprocity of feelings, she is almost on the verge of neurotic breakdown. And it is here that technique comes in. How to describe the mind of a neurotic woman is the challenge before the novelist and she tackles it skilfully with success. She does it by making use of the weird animal imagery which suggests her disturbed state of mind. Such imagery is to be seen in contrast to the majestic image of the peacock which is the central symbol of the novel as suggested by the title. This is an instance of the relationship between theme and technique. A prophecy made in Maya's childhood about a tragic event in the fourth year of her married life plays a very important role in the novel. This prophecy haunts Maya's mind and the prophecy is used as leitmotif which is a term of music but has come to critical vocabulary in literature. This is another instance of technique in the novel.

Her second novel *Voices in the City* is a novel about a family and the influence of the city of Calcutta on the three characters of the family, namely, Nirode, Monisha and Amla. The novel makes use of symbolism specially in the context of the city of Calcutta and how it affects the lives of the three-character mentioned above. Monisha, like many of Anita Desai's heroines, is sensitive and a vicitim of ill-matched marriage. She is an intellectual and fond of reading, but nobody in the joint family, including her husband, appreciates her tastes, nor does she get privacy. She is an example of a maladjusted woman who is an introvert by nature. The question of technique comes when such a character is to be portrayed in a novel. Anita Desai appropriately chooses the method of using her diary as the medium to portray her. And this is a very natural method because a character like Monisha who moves to share and reciprocate her feelings finds diary-writings as an outlet for her suppressed feelings. And that is why the section devoted to her is entitled "Monisha : Her Diary." She also records her reaction to the city of Calcutta. The whole novel is divided into four sections, namely, "Nirode," "Monisha", "Amla", and "Mother". Keeping in view the title of the novel the fourth section devoted to the mother is not so relevant because she does not live in the city of Calcutta and comes here only to attend Monisha's funeral who has committed suicide by self-immolation. The novel also makes use of some poems although they are not very significant from thematic point of view. An important fictional technique in the novel is to describe a dream of Nirode which is about his dead father, his mother and himself. This device is used effectively for describing Nirode's ccomplicated ambivalent relationship with his parents. This is an instance of fictional technique used to portray the psyche of Nirode. What could not be described through Nirode's action is partly described through his sub-conscious feelings with the help of a dream.

Anita Desai's third novel *Bye-Bye Black Bird* is a novel about Indian immigrants settled in London focusing attention on three characters 'Dev', "Adit", and 'Sarah'. The theme of the novel is the life and the feelings of these immigrants in a foreign country particularly in the context of Sarah and her mis-matched marriage with a black Indian which results in many agonising moments. the title of the novel refers to Adit's final farewell to Asian immigrants in England when he leaves

England for India for good. As compared to her two earlier novels *Bye-Bye Black Bird* is not so important from psychological point of view. In this novel it is her descriptive prose and use of rhetoric that is significant from the point of view of technique. Dev's harangue, when he is proselytising about the reversal of the historical fact of cultural colonisation, is an example of Anita Desai's rhetorical use of language. But even more important is the fact that here the technique is used to describe Dev's character, his attitude towards British and their superciliousness. For the most part of the novel he remains anti-British pretending to be a cultural ambassador of India to England. But later, he takes after the character of Adit and becomes an Anglophile. Anita Desai uses irony when such a reversal of role comes and it becomes an effective technique to describe the hollowness of Dev's character. All his criticism and contempt for the British and his pretended love for India disappears in thin air. The novel uses poems at several places for different purposes but mainly to describe some aspect of the characters. Sarah's mental confusion is also well described at the end of part one when her hypnogogic mind is described. She tries her best to understand and accept Indian culture and music but she fails and this is an example of Desai's skill in taking us into the mind of Sarah.

Where Shall We Go This Summer ? is once again a family drama focusing attention on Sita, a housewife who is pregnant but hates to deliver the baby. She is hypersensitive and is emotionally so charged and so irrational that she becomes a burden and a source of annoyance to her children and husband. Psychological probing is there mainly into the character of Sita describing how she is never able to come out of the fantasy world of her childhood. The novel uses symbolism to describe Sita's psyche through the symbol of wounded eagle. The title of the novel is not very significant and it is just a casual question for affluent families as to which holiday resort they would go during the summer.The novel is divided into three sections, namely : ''Monsoon '67'', ''Winter '47'', and ''Monsoon '67''. This, structural division is related to three stages in the development of Sita's character during the course of the novel. Section one describes her life in Bombay and by implication her contact with reality, the second section describes her escape from reality to the world of fantasy, magic and miracle, and the last section is concerned her return to Bombay which is by implication her return to the world of reality.

The island city dichotomy is symbolic of the world of fantasy and reality. The novel also makes use of poetry in a very significant manner. As in *Clear Light of Day*, here also, poetry offers a vision of life. The

Cavafy poem mentally prepares Sita to accept reality, and D.H. Lawrence's poem, lines of which she has been trying to recollect, gives her solution and the solution is that life must go on with our duties discharged and responsibilities borne. Here the technique of using poetry is the medium through which the final point is reached in the novel.

Fire on the Mountain is also a family drama and this time it covers many generations but the focus is on Nanda Kaul, the widow of a vice-chancellor, through whose point of view primarily the story has been narrated. The other important character is that of Raka the great grand-child of Nanda Kaul. This novel too is a study of feminine psyche but here the canvas is bigger in that it includes both an old woman and a girl. The flashback technique has been used which is but natural since the novel focuses on the character of Nanda Kaul who is living in isolation in a secluded bunglow in Kasauli along with a male servant. The novel makes use of symbolism to portray the character of Nanda Kaul and Raka and it is mainly through nature imagery that symbolism is used. The bare mountainous terrain and a desert burnt out bunglow at hill-top which fascinates Raka symbolises her emotionally void character which is a result of her emotional deprivation since she comes from a broken home with a sick mother and an alcoholic father who beats his wife. The novel also makes use of poetry though not in a very significant manner. The title refers to the last act in the novel by Raka when she sets the forest on fire. The pyromania of Raka is the result of her maladjusted personality because of her unhealthy upbringing at home where there was no parental love and affection.

Clear Light of Day is also a family drama covering two generations of Das family but mainly dealing with the second generation, that is of the children — Bim, Tara, Raja and Baba. The novel covers two historical periods of India, one of freedom struggle and another of independence. The story is primarly narrated from Bim's point of view who is the most important character in the novel. She sacrifices her whole life for her siblings, educating them and marrying them, taking care of mentally-retarded Baba and senile Mira Masi since she was the eldest of the family and the father had died. The novel is also a study in feminine psyche, not only that of girls and women but also of an old woman. The novel has two epigraphs,one referring to memory and another to the passage of time. Time plays an important role in the novel and what is implied as elucidated by Anita Desai herself is that time passes but things remain the same except that the pattern changes. Perhaps she is referring to eternal varieties of life and to the fact that human nature does not change. A singnificant technique employed in the novel is the use of poetry in the context of Raja and Bim. In Raja's case it is natural since he is very fond of Urdu poetry and in Bim's case the poems quoted are related to her character and they reflect her feelings and thoughts. But the most significant use of poetry is to be found at the end of the novel when two couplets of Iqbal, set to music, provide the ultimate vision of the novel and by implication this is the clear light of the day that dawns upon Bim making her way clear, despelling all her confusion and giving her a philosophy of life. Besides the use of poetry, music to which it is set, makes it more effective. In her other novels too Anita Desai has made use of music. For example, in *Bye-Bye Black Bird, Where Shall We Go This Summer?* and *Voices in the City* but nowhere so effectively as in this novel. Here music has been used as a technique and elsewhere it is either incidental or a part of the atmosphere. In *Bye-Bye Black Bird* a music soiree is a part of get-together function for Indians and their effort to create mini-India in London. In the same novel Adit listens to sitar music on gramophone to be in touch with Indian culture.

In Custody is a novel dealing with two characters, that of Deven and Nur. Deven is a teacher of Hindi but fond of Urdu literature and is a great fan of Nur, a very famous Urdu poet. From the technique point of view the most important thing is the implications of the title. There are authorial comments about the title meaning that Nur's poetry would be in safe custody of Deven but the irony is that he is in the custody of Nur's personality and his unending irrational demands as though Deven were responsible for every trouble in Nur's life. His letters keep pouring to Deven asking for money for various purposes. Deven's anguish has been well described through a nightmarish vision that he has at the end of the novel as described in Chapter Five of the book. This novel also makes use of poetry but ironically none of the poems quoted are by Nur. Curiously enough, they are poems by Shelley and Keats which suggests the romantic nature of Nur's poetry and his refusal to accept the reality of the present. Even though living in recent times, mentally he lives in the day of Rajas and Zamindars of pre-independence India as shown in his babblings to Deven. The use of poetry in the novel is not so significant as in case of *Clear Light of Day* or *Where Shall We Go This Summer?* Nevertheless, it is not to tally irrelevant, because as seen above, it throws light on Nur's character. From the point of view of characterisation we notice that the unheroic character of Deven has been described effectively which may stand for an average middle class man striving hard to live life. And his character becomes all the more pitiable since he is married to an uneducated woman who is miles away from literature. The novel has an open ending which suggests the eternal troubles in the life of this insignificant teacher.

Her latest novel *Baumgartner's Bombay* has the theme of the plight of a displaced person who is the hero of the novel. Hugo Baumgartner is a Jew who is advised to leave Germany at the rise of Nazism and he comes to the British India before the Second World War to begin his new life. The title of the novel refers to the hero's experience of Bombay because after independence he lived in Bombay. The novel covers a long period of time beginning from Baumgartner's childhood in Berlin and coming down to his murder in Circa, the late 60s or early 70s. The novel focuses on Baumgartner but there are other characters also all of whom are connected with him. It is the story of a rootless, homeless and familyless man always trying to belong, wanting to be accepted but never accepted. The pathos of the novel lies in the fact that even after living for almost fifty years in India he is not accepted by Indian society and to engage himself he picks up stray and wounded cats and keeps them in his flat but the unfeeling world calls him *Billiwala Pagal.* The novel uses flashback technique through which we are informed of his childhood. There are several German songs and poems used in the novel justifiably since he is a German. Some of these poems belong to his childhood days which he recollects with nostalgia. But the German patriotic song, sung by German citizens imprisoned with him, has greater significance in that even though he is a victim of Nazi Germany yet he has to sing along with others.On linguistic level the novel effectively transcribes different varieties of English as spoken by Indians, and the British. Certain Hindi words are also used in the novel to give realistic effect, for example when he is being taken on a train to Ahmed Nagar we hear the calls of *Garam Chai.*

The novel has an epigraph from T.S. Eliot's poem "East Coker" which signifies the rise and the fall of families. Certainly, we have seen the prosperity of Baumgartner's family and his impoverished state in the novel but there is no suggestion of being "restored" to his earlier prosperity. The novel is interspersed with several German words which is but natural since the hero is a German and there are certain other German characters also in the novel. At the same time, there is also use of Hindi words like *Parikarma* or the Mohurram chant "Hassan-Husain-Hassan-Hussain. From the technique point of view, another noticeable thing is the novelist's realistic descriptions of places, for example, that of Benaras. We do not know if the novelist had ever visited Benaras but her description is faithful.

Thus we find that Anita Desai in her different novels has written about different themes, some of them are common and even overlapping. In doing so she makes use of different fictional techniques and uses them for narrating the story effectively. She may not be a technical innovator, but her use of poetry is not something very common. One thing is sure that she makes use of various fictional techniques with success and they are always in accordance with the demands of the novel and if one could use an analogy from textile, the theme is warp and the technique is woof. With the blend of the two comes out a tapestry that is Anita Desai's fiction.

BIBLIOGRAPHICAL NOTE

The Bibliography is broadly divided into the Primary and the Secondary sources. The Primary Sources are further divided into (i) The Novels; (ii) The Short Stories; (iii) The Uncollected Short Stories; (iv) Children's Literature; and (v) Essays, Articles, Reviews and Interviews by Anita Desai.

The first section of the secondary sources lists book-length critical studies on the fiction of Anita Desai. The second section lists Articles, Essay and Reviews on the works of Anita Desai. The third section lists a few of the important studies related to Fiction in general and literary criticism concerning that Fiction in general. No claim is made that this Bibliography is complete, However, an attempt has definitely been made to represent Anita Desai's scholarship.

BIBLIOGRAPHY

PRIMARY SOURCES

Novels

Cry the Peacock, London: Peter Owen, 1963; Delhi, Orient Paperbacks, 1986.

Voices in the City, London: Peter Owen, 1965; Delhi, Orient Paperbacks, 1965.

Bye-Bye Black Bird, Delhi, Hind Pocket Books, 1971; Delhi, Orient Paperbacks, 1985.

Where Shall We Go This Summer? Delhi, Vikas Publications, 1975; Delhi, Orient Paperbacks, 1982.

Fire on the Mountain, London, William Heinemann, 1977; New Delhi, Allied Publishers, 1977.

Clear Light of Day, London, William Heinemann, 1980; New Delhi, Allied Publishers, 1980.

In Custody, London, William Heinemann, 1984.

Baumgartner's Bombay, London, William Heinemann, 1988; Penguin Books, 1989.

Short Stories

Games at Twilight, London, William Heinemann, 1982; Delhi, Allied Publishers, 1978.

Uncollected Short Stories

"Circus Cat, Alley," Delhi, *Thought,* 1957. Collected in M.C. Gabriel and Gwen Gabriel, eds., *A Selection of Modern Indian Short Stories,* Delhi, Sidhartha Publications, 1968, pp. 95-98.

"Tea with the Maharani," *Envoy,* Vol. 4, Nos. 3-4, Jan.-Feb., 1959, pp. 22-23 and 32.

"Grand Mother," *Writers Workshop Miscellany,* Vol. I, Aug. 1960, pp. 1-10.

"An Examination," *Writers Workshop Miscellany,* Vol. III, 1960.

"Mr. Bose's Private Bliss," *Envoy,* Vol. 6,Nos. 7-8, May-June, 1961, pp. 16-17.

"Ghost House," *Quest,* No. 28, Jan.-March, 1961.

"Descent from the Roof-top," *The Illustrated Weekly of India,* 91(1), 4 Jan., 1970, pp. 36-39.

Children's Literature

The Peacock Garden, Bombay, India Book House, 1974, London, William Heinemann, 1979.

Cat on a Houseboat, Bombay, Orient Longmans, 1976.

The Village by the Sea, London, William Heinemann, 1982; Delhi, Allied Publishers, 1985.

Essays, Articles, Reviews, Interviews

"Women Writers," *Quest,* No. 65, April/June, 1970, pp. 39-42.

"The Indian Writers' Problems," *The Literary Criterion,* Vol. XI, No. 4, Autumn 1975, pp. 29-32.

"Jhabvala : A sure Winner," *The Illustrated Weekly of India,* March 7, 1976, p. 6.

"Book Review of *Hymns in Darkness* by Nissim Ezekiel, " *The IPEN,* March-April 1977, No. 3-4.

"Book I Enjoyed Writing Most," *Contemporary Indian Literature,* Vol. 13, No. 4, October-December 1973, pp. 23-24.

"The Timid Movement of a Wing," *The Indian Literary Review,* Vol. I, No. 4, August 1978, pp. 11-13.

"Within and Without Tradition," *ACLALS Newsletter,* April 5, 1979, pp. 5-21.

"Memoirs of a Mendicant Professor, A Review," *Quest*, No. 66, July-September, 1970.

"Out of the Shadows," *The Indian Express,* June 10, 1984.

"Reply to the Questionnaire," *Kakatiya Journal of English Studies,* Vol. III, No. 1 (1978), pp. 1-6.

"An Interview with Anita Desai," by Yashodara Dalmia, *The Times of India,* April 29, 1979.

"Anita Desai : Interview by Jasbir Jain," *Rajasthan University Studies in English,* Vol. XII, 1979, pp. 61-69.

"An Interview with Anita Desai," by Atma Ram, *World Literature Written in English,* Vol. XVI, No. 1, April 1977, pp. 95-104.

"Tremendous Changes," Interview by Sunil Sethi, *India Today,* December 15, 1980.

"Anita Desai at Work : An Interview," by Ramesh K. Srivastava, *Perspectives on Anita Desai,* ed., Ramesh K. Srivastava, Ghaziabad, Vimal Prakashan, 1984.

"It's Fatal to Write with an Audience in Mind," An Interview by Ketaki Sheth, *Imprint*, June 1984.

"Silent Spaces of Inner Vastness : Meet the Author," by Madhushree Sinha Roy, *The Times of India,* June 18, 1992, p. 7.

SECONDARY SOURCES

Critical Studies on Anita Desai

Books

Bande, Usha, *The Novels of Anita Desai : A Study in Character and Conflict.*, New Delhi, Prestige Books, 1988.

Belliappa, Meena, *Anita Desai : A Study of Her Fiction,* Calcutta, Writers Workshop Publication, 1971.

Dhawan, R.K. Ed., *The Fiction of Anita Desai,* New Delhi, Bahri Publications, 1989.

—, *Indian Women Novelists,* Set I, Vol. II, New Delhi, Prestige Books, 1991.

Jain, Jasbir, *Stairs to the Attic : The Novels of Anita Desai,* Jaipur, Printwell Publishers, 1987.

Jena, Seema, *Voices and Vision of Anita Desai,* New Delhi, Ashish Publishing House, 1989.

Pathania, Usha, *Human Bonds and Bondages : The Fiction of Anita Desai and Kamala Markandeya,* Delhi, Kanishka Publishing House.

Prasad, Madhusudan, *Anita Desai : The Novelist,* Allahabad, New Horizon, 1981.

Rao, B. Ramachandra, *The Novels of Mrs. Anita Desai : A Study,* New Delhi, Kalyani Publishers, 1977.

Sharma, R.S., *Anita Desai,* New Delhi, Arnold Heinemann, 1981.

Srivastava, Ramesh K. Ed., *Perspectives on Anita Desai,* Ghaziabad, Vimal Prakashan, 1984.

Tripathi, J.P., *The Mind and Art of Anita Desai,* Bareilly, Prakash Book Depot, 1986.

Articles, Essays, Reviews

Acharya, Shanta, ''Problems of Self in the Novels of Anita Desai,'' *Explorations in Modern Indo-English Fiction,* Ed. R.K. Dhawan, New Delhi, Bahri Publications, 1982, pp. 236-54.

Aithal, S. Krishnamoorthy and Rashmi Aithal, '' East-West Encounter in Four Indo-English Novels, '' *ACLALS Bulletin,* Sixth Series, No. 1, November 1982, pp. 1-16.

Alcock, Peter. ''Rope, Serpent, Fire : Recent Fiction of Anita Desai,'' *The Journal of Indian Writing in English,* Vol. IX, No. 1 January 1981, pp. 15-34.

Amin, Amin, ''Imagery as a Mode of Apprehension in Anita Desai's Novel,'' *Littcrit,* Vol. X, No. 1, 1984, pp. 36-45.

Asnani, Shyam M. ''Anita Desai's Fiction : A New Dimension,'' *Indian Literature,* Vol. XXIV, No. 2, March-April 1981, pp. 44-54.

—, ''Theme of Withdrawal and Loneliness in Anita Desai's *Fire on the Mountain,* '' *The Journal of Indian Writing in English,* Vol. IX, No. 1, Jan. 81, pp. 81-92.

—, ''Anita Desai: The Novelist with Unique Personal Vision'', *Contemporary Indian Thought,* Vol. 14, No. 1, January-March, 1974, pp. 6-9, 16-21.

Banerjee, Purabi, ''Bookworm's Progress,'' *The Statesman,* April 10, 1983.

Daftry, Mayana, ''Review of *Cry the Peacock*'', *Quest,* Vol. 10, No. 1, Winter 1983, p. 50.

Daruwalla, Keki N., ''Built on a Non-Issue — Review of *In Custody,* '' *The Hindustan Times,* January 13, 1985.

Dua, M.R, ''Anita Desai,'' *Femina,* January 4, 1974, p. 25.

Dubashi, Jagannath, "*The Village by the Sea* : An Indian Family Story — A Review," *India Today*, April 15, 1983.

Dudt, Charmazel, "Past and Present : A Journey to Confrontation," *The Journal of Indian Writing in English*, Vol. IX, No. 1, January 1981, pp. 67-73 (A Study of *Where Shall We Go This Summer ?*)

Ganguli, Chandra, "*Fire on the Mountain* : An Analysis," *Critical Quarterly*, December 6, 1981, pp. 40-44.

Gabriele, A., "Anita Desai's *Fire on the Mountain* : A Review," *Times Literary Supplement*, June 17, 1977, p. 721.

Glendinning, Victoria, "Mood Indigo, Review of *Games at Twilight and other Stories*," *Times Literary Supplement*, September 1, 1978, p. 973.

Goyal, Bhagat S., "The World of Women Novelists," *The Hindustan Times Weekly*, Vol. 4, No. 12, 69, pp. 64-69.

Hope, Mary, "Review of Anita Desai's *Games at Twilight*," *Spectator*, July 22, 1978, p. 24.

Iyengar, K.R.S., "A Note on Anita Desai's Novels," *Banasthali* Patrika, No. 12, January 1969, pp. 64-69.

Jain, Jasbir, "Anita Desai," *Indo-English Novelists*, Ed. Madhusudan Prasad, New Delhi, Sterling Publishers, 1982, pp. 23-50.

—, "The Use of Fantasy in Anita Desai's Novels," *Explorations in Modern Indo-English Fiction*, ed. R.K. Dhawan, New Delhi : Bahri Publications, 1982, pp. 227-237.

—, "Anita Desai: The Woman and the Novelist," *The Journal of Indian Writing in English*, The Special Number, Vol. IX, Christian University, Texas.

Kohli, Suresh, "Indian Women Novelists in English," *Times Weekly*, November 8, 1970, p. 3.

Krishna Francine E., "A Lulled Life — A Review of *Where Shall We Go This Summer?*" *Quest*, No. 99, January-February 1976, pp. 90-91.

—, "Anita Desai: *Fire on The Mountain*," *Indian Literature*, Vol. 25, No. 5, September-October 1982, pp. 43-46.

Lal, P. "Review of *Voices in the City*," *Littcrit*, Vol. 2, December 1976, pp. 51-53.

—, "Review of *Cry the Peacock*", *The Nagpur Times*, December 15, 1968.

—, "Review of *Cry the Peacock,*" *Times Literary Supplement,* No. 3, 182, Friday, February 22, 1963.

Maini, D.S., "*Cry the Peacock* as a Poetic Novel," *English Literature of the Past Fifty Years,* 1917-67, Ed. Narasimhaiah, Mysore, Mysore University, 1970, pp. 225-34.

—, "Achievement of Anita Desai," *Indo-English Literature,* ed. K.K. Sharma, Ghaziabad, Vimal Prakashan, 1977, p. 215-30.

Malhotra, M.L., "Anita Desai : A Writer with a Promise," in *Bridges of Literature,* Ajmer, Sunanda Publication, 1971, pp. 205-22.

Masilamani, J.G., "Feminism in Anita Desai," *Kakatiya Journal of English Studies,* 3, 1978, pp. 25-33.

Mukherjee, Meenakshi. "A Review of *Bye-Bye Black Bird*", *Quest,* No. 75, March-April, 1972, pp. 97-98.

—, "The Theme of Displacement in Anita Desai and Kamala Markandeya," *World Literature Written in English,* Vol. XVII, No. 1, 1978, pp. 225-235.

Narasimhan, Raji, "Desai *vs.* Desani," *Indian Literature,* Nos. 3-4, July-December 1975, 180-84.

Pandey, Mrinal, "Women Without Men, Review of *Fire on the Mountain,*" *The Times of India,* December 18, 1977, p. 2.

Parasuram, Laxmi, "Mountain : A New Dimension of Feminine Self-perception," *Literary Criterion,* Vol. XVI, No. 3, 1981, pp. 58-64.

Prasad, Hari Mohan, "Sound or Sense: A Study of Anita Desai's *Bye-Bye Black Bird,*" *Journal of Indian Writing in English,* Vol. IX, No. 1, January 1981, pp. 51-66.

Prasad, Madhusudan, "*Where Shall We Go This Summer?* : A Critical Study," *Rajasthan Journal of English Studies,* 13-14, 1981, pp. 62-68.

Rathi, R.P., "Review of the Village by the Sea", *Indian and Foreign Review,* September 1-15, 1983.

Rao, B. Ramachandra, "Anita Desai : Themes and Variations in the Novels and Short Stories of Anita Desai", *Journal of Literature and Aesthetics,* Vol. II, No. 2 and 3, 1982, pp.74-79.

Rao, Maithili, "Landscape of the Mind", *Eves Weekly,* August 6, 1983, pp. 52-55.

Rueben, Elizabeth, "Anita Desai's *Fire on the Mountain*", *World Literature Written in English,* Vol. XVII, No. 1, April, 1978.

Rao, Vimala "*Where Shall We Go This Summer?*: An Analysis", *Commonwealth Quarterly,* Vol. 3, No. 9, December 1978.

—, "Four Women Novelists and their Concern with the Indian Element", *Journal of Mysore University* (Humanities), Summer 1965, pp. 8-16.

Ram, Atma, "Anita Desai", *The National Herald,* June 26, 1980.

Ram, Atma, "Exploration of Inner Sensibility", *Perspective,* July 1978, pp. 54-55.

—, "Anita Desai : The Novelist who Writes for Herself", *The Journal of Indian Writing in English,* Vol. V, No. 2, July, 1977, pp. 39-42.

—, "Indians slow to Recognise Talent in their Midst", *The Tribune,* June 26, 1977.

—, "Island on the Island : Anita Desai's *Where Shall We Go This Summer?*" *World Literature Written in English,* No. 2, November 1976, pp. 381-83.

Sethi, Sunil, "Pieces of the Past, Review of Anita Desai's *Clear Light of Day*", *India Today,* 5, No. 23, December 1-15, 1980, pp. 142-43.

Sharma, R.S., "Alienation, Accommodation and the Locale in Anita Desai's *Bye-Bye Black Bird*", *Literary Criterion,* Vol. 14, No. 4, 1979, pp. 31-49.

—, "Mother and the City : Archetypes in Anita Desai's *Voices in the City*", *Journal of Literary Studies,* Vol. 2, No. 2, December 1979, pp. 57-77.

Shastri, N.R., "*Where Shall We Go This Summer?*: A Critical Study", *Osmania Journal of English Studies,* Vol. 17, 1981, pp. 83-103.

Singh, Brijraj, "The Fiction of Anita Desai", *The Humanities Review,* Vol. 3, No. 2, July-December 1981, pp. 40-43.

Sivaramakrishna, M., "From Alienation to Mythic Acceptance : The Ordeal of Consciousness in Anita Desai's Fiction", *Kakatiya Journal of English Studies,* Vol. III, No. 1, 1978, pp. 7-24.

Sunwani, V.K., "Carignano : A Quiet Place", *Journal of Literary Studies,* Vol. II, No. 2, December 1979, pp. 79-92.

T. Vijay Kumar, "Review of *In Custody,*" *Indian Book Chronicle,* 10, Nos. 17-18, September 1-10,? pp. 286-87.

Varady, Evelyn, "American and British Responses and Anita Desai's *Games at Twilight and other Stories*", *Journal of Indian Writing in English*, Vol. VIII, No. 1-2, January-July, 1982, pp. 27-34.

Vyas, B.O., "Viscid Voices of the Inner Kingdom", *The Journal of Indian Writing in English*, Vol. IX, No.1, January 1981.

Weir, Ann Lowry, "The Illusion of Maya : Feminine Consciousness in Anita Desai's *Cry the Peacock*", *Journal of South Asian Literature*, Vol. XVI, No. 2, 1981, pp. 1-4.

—, "Anita Desai's *Fire on the Mountain*", *World Literature Written in English*, Vol. VII, No. 2, November 1978, pp. 548-50.

BACKGROUND STUDIES AND OTHER BOOKS CONSULTED

Bhatnagar, K.C., *Realism in Major Indo-English Fiction.*, Bareilly, Prakash Book Depot, 1980.

Brooks, Jr., Cleanth and Robert Penn Warren, *Understanding Fiction* (New, Appleton Century — Crofts. Inc. 1948), p. 570.

Brunton, T.D., "India in Fiction : The Heritage of Indianness", *Critical Essays on Indian Writing in English,* Eds. Naik, Desai, Amur, Dharwar, Karnataka University, 1968.

Dhawan, R.K. (Ed.), *Explorations in Modern Indo-English Fiction,* New Delhi, Bahri Publication, 1982.

Dobrenkov, V.I., *Neo-Freudians in Search of Truth,* Moscow, Progress Publishers, 1976.

Forster, E.M., *Aspects of the Novel,* London, Penguin Books, 1979.

Fruend, Phillip, *The Art of Reading Novels,* New York, Collier Books, 1966, p. 233.

Fry, Northrop, *Anatomy of Criticism,* Princeton, Princeton University Press, 1973.

Gokak, V.K., *English in India : Its Present and Future,* Bombay, Asia Publishing House, 1964.

Harrex, S.C., The Fire and the Offering : *The English Language Novel of India,* 1935-1970, Calcutta, Writers Workshop, 1977.

— *The Modern Novel in English,* Calcutta, Writers Workshop, 1971.

Heller, Erich. *The Disinherited Mind,* Edinburgh, Penguin Books, 1961.

Hemenway, Stephen I, *The Novel of India : Vol. II, The Indo-Anglian Novel,* Calcutta, Writers Workshop, 1975.

Iyengar, K.R.S., *Indian Writing in English,* New Delhi, Sterling Publishers, 1984.

James Henry, "The Art of Fiction," *American Literature of 19th Century : An Anthology* (India, Eurasia Publishing House, 1965).

Kalinnikova, Elena, J., *Indian English Literature: : A Perspective.* Ghaziabad, Vimal Prakashan, 1982.

Krishnaswamy, Shantha, *The Women in Indian Fiction in English,* New Delhi, Ashish Publishing House, 1984.

Kumar, Suman, *The Fictional Art of Somerset Maugham,* Varanasi, Kashividyapeeth Publications, 1977.

Lal, P., *The Concept of an Indian Literature,* Calcutta, Writers Workshop, 1969.

Maslow, A.H., *Motivation and Personality,* New York, Harper and Brothers Publishers, 1954.

Mehta, P.P., *Indo-Anglian Fiction : An Assessment,* Bareilly, Prakash Book Depot, 1968.

Mukherjee, Meenakshi, "*The Twice-Born Fiction : Themes and Techniques of the Indian Novel in English,* New Delhi, Arnold Heinemann, 1971.

—, *Consideration*, Ed., New Delhi, Allied Publishers, 1977.

Naik, M.K., *Aspects of Indian Writing in English* , New Delhi, Macmilian, 1979.

—, *A History of Indian English Literature,* New Delhi, Sahitya Akademi, 1982.

Naik, M.K., Desai, S.K. and Amur, G.S. Eds., *Critical Essays on Indian Writing in English,* Dharwar, Karnataka University, 1968.

—, *Dimensions of Indian English Literature,* New Delhi, Sterling Publishers, 1984.

—, *Perspectives on Indian Fiction in English,* New Delhi, Abhinav Publications, 1985.

—, *Studies in Indian English Literature*, New Delhi, SterlingPublishers, 1987.

Narasimhaiah, C.D., *The Swan and the Eagle,* Simla, Indian Institute of Advanced Study, 1969.

Narasimhaiah, C.D. Ed., *Indian Literature of the Past Fifty Years (1917-1967),* Mysore, University of Mysore, 1970.

—, *Fiction and Reading Public in India,* Mysore, University of Mysore, 1977.

—, *Awakened Conscience : Studies in Commonwealth Literature,* New Delhi, Sterling Publishers, 1978.

Narasimhan, Raji, *Sensibility Under Stress,* New Delhi, Ashajanak Prakashan, 1976.

Page, James D., *Abnormal Psychology,* New Delhi, McGraw Hill Book Company, Inc., 1947.

Parameswaran, Uma, *A Study of Representative Indo-English Novelists,* New Delhi, Vikas Publishing House, 1975.

Pathak, R.S., *Indian Fiction in English: Problems and Promises,* New Delhi, Northern Book Centre, 1990.

Pradhan, N.S. Ed., *Major Indian Novels,* New Delhi, Arnold Heinmann, 1985.

Prasad, Hari Mohan Ed., *Response : Recent Revelations of Indian Fiction in English,* Bareilly, Prakash Book Depot, 1983.

Punekar-Mokashi S., *The Indo-Anglian Creed and Allied Essays,* Calcutta, Writers Workshop, 1972.

Radhakrishnan, N., *Indo-Anglian Fiction : Major Trends and Themes,* Madras, Emerald Publishers, 1984.

Raghavacharyulu, D.V.K. Ed., *The Critical Response,* Madras, Macmilian, 1980.

Raizada, Harish, *The Lotus and the Rose : Indian Fiction in English,* 1857—1947, Aligarh, Faculty of Arts, Aligarh Muslim University, 1978.

Ram, Atma, *Essays on Indian English Literature,* Aurangabad, Parimal Prakashan, 1984.

Ramamurty, K.S., *Rise of the Indian Novel in English,* New Delhi, Sterling Publishers, 1987.

Rank, Otto, *The Writer's Creative Individuality and the Development of Literature,* Moscow, Express Publishers, 1977.

Read, Herbert, *Collected Essays on Criticism,* London, Faber and Faber Ltd., 1950, p. 19.